P9-EGN-330

WITHDRAWN

Kelly Library

3 ──── 0150 6

		PRINTED IN U. S. A.	⁹⁄₆₅
			FEB 4 '85
			FEB 4 '85
			MAR 6 '72
			N I
			OCT 24 '69
			E H
			NOV 13 '68
			FEB 18 '68
			NO3 0 '67
			NO 15 '67
			MY 16 '65
			DE
			JUN 13
			AP 26 '63
			MR 11 '63
			FE 19 '6
			FE 6 '63

Date Due

EMORY AND HENRY LIBRARY

THE AMERICAN APPROACH
TO FOREIGN POLICY

Revised Edition

THE AMERICAN APPROACH
TO FOREIGN POLICY

Dexter Perkins

HARVARD
UNIVERSITY
PRESS

Cambridge

1962

© Copyright 1962 by the President and Fellows
of Harvard College • All rights reserved •
Distributed in Great Britain by Oxford
University Press, London • Library of Congress
Catalog Card Number: 62–11400 • Printed in the
United States of America

E 183.7
P46

Foreword
to the Revised Edition

THESE essays, written eleven years ago, have had so favorable a reception as to warrant a revision. They have been translated into eight languages and therefore have had readers outside the United States where the spirit and the mechanics of American foreign policy are not always understood. Never was such understanding more necessary than today, and I hope that I have contributed something to it. For the rest I let stand the comments contained in the 1951 foreword.

Once again I express my deep appreciation for the opportunity afforded me by the Gottesman Foundation to deliver these lectures in their original form at Uppsala University in 1949, and record my gratitude for the encouragement and sympathetic interest which I met with from Mr. Gottesman himself. I wish also to acknowledge with warmth the friendly reception accorded me by the Rector of the University, Professor Berg, whose hospitality was most cordial.

In assessing the American Secretaries of State, I asked for the opinion of a number of well-known scholars in the

[v]

84076

WITHDRAWN

EMORY AND HENRY LIBRARY

FOREWORD

field of American diplomatic history. I, therefore, gratefully record the cooperation of Professors T. A. Bailey, Ruhl J. Bartlett, Samuel Flagg Bemis, Richard W. Leopold, Julius W. Pratt, J. Fred Rippy, Louis M. Sears, Graham Stuart, and Arthur P. Whitaker.

I asked Mr. Sumner Welles to give me the benefit of his learning and wide experience with regard to certain passages in Chapter VIII and am grateful for his prompt and cordial assistance.

In the preparation of this book I have used certain materials drawn from my previous writings, and I wish to thank the *Yale Review* for permission to repeat some paragraphs from an article on "The American Attitude towards War," and Oxford University Press for similar permission to quote from my book, "The Evolution of American Foreign Policy."

In the preparation of the manuscript for the press, I had the services of my secretary, Miss Marjorie Gilles, who was much more than a mere amanuensis. Her intense and critical interest in the project, her devoted service along many different lines, are not to be measured by any form of words.

Rochester, New York   DEXTER PERKINS
February 1962

Contents

{ vii }

I

The Broad Picture
1789-1945

———◆·◄◉►·◆———

THE foreign policy of the United States has almost always been considered from what may fairly be called
the chronological point of view. It has rarely been treated
topically and with reference to broad areas of thought. In
these essays it is the latter approach which will be pursued.
It seems wise, however, to begin by briefly outlining the
course of American diplomacy and to indicate what have
been the main themes of American action in the field of
international affairs from the beginnings to the Second
World War. The story may be conveniently divided into
two major periods, the period before and that after 1898.
In the first of these two periods, three broad lines of development may be traced: the evolution of the isolationist
viewpoint as regards Europe, the rise and growth of the
principle of the Monroe Doctrine as regards our relations
with the New World, and the process of expansion from
the original territorial limits of the United States to a truly
continental domain. In the second period, the scope of
American action widens. In the East, in Europe, and in the
Americas there are great movements which may be con-

sidered in turn and which bring us to the portentous role exercised by the United States today. Of course the division between these two epochs is not as sharp as the selection of a given date like 1898 would make it appear. From time to time, in the recounting of the story, we may be compelled to go a little further forward or backward to understand fully the events with which we deal. But the division is in the main a sound one, based on that awakening to a sense of national power that undoubtedly followed upon the war with Spain. It has a significance that cannot be denied.

Let us then, first of all, examine the early years of the republic from the point of view of the isolationist philosophy which has played so large a role in American diplomatic history. The existence of this philosophy is easy enough to explain, at the outset. After all, the Americans were provincials, separated from Europe by a wide ocean and preoccupied with the task of developing a continent. The Revolution itself was an act of isolation, a cutting of the ties with the Old World, the deed of a society which felt itself different from those which existed on the other side of the Atlantic and which was, indeed, unique in its composition and in its aspirations. It is not strange, therefore, that even in the extreme need of the moment the alliance with France, signed on February 6, 1778, was accepted reluctantly. The war was no sooner over than suspicions of the purposes of the French government began to arise, and a desire to wriggle out of the alliance made itself manifest. This desire was naturally strengthened by the outbreak of the French Revolutionary wars in Europe in the early 90's. For American opinion on the great European conflict was sharply divided, and it was elementary wisdom not to weaken the structure of the new government set up under the Constitution by any policy of foreign adventure.

The Washington administration chose the course of strict neutrality. Even so, it had its difficulties. There were bitter disputes over questions of foreign policy, and an attempted liquidation of various matters of controversy with Great Britain brought down on the head of the President a torrent of abuse from the sympathizers with France. The factionalism of these years, however, and the shameless interference of the French ministers in American domestic affairs further convinced Washington of the wisdom of his course, and, in the famous Farewell Address of September 17, 1796, he laid down the principle that we should have as little political connection as possible with European states, avoiding partiality for one or resentment against another and shaping our policy on the basis of our own interest alone. True, the President qualified his general principle, admitting the possibility of extraordinary alliances for extraordinary emergencies. But the general tenor of what he had to say was more important than the exception which, with sound judgment, he put forward, and it was the general tenor which exercised a long-time influence over the policies of the United States.

Shortly after 1796, the arrogant treatment by the French government of American commerce, and of the American envoys sent to seek an accommodation of differences, involved the country in an informal war upon the seas with France. This war led to the abrogation of the treaty of alliance of revolutionary days, and from that time forward, until the momentous agreement of January 1, 1942, at the beginning of American participation in the Second World War, the United States never entered into close political association with any European power. True, there were occasions when such an association was considered, especially in the administration of Thomas Jefferson and again in connection with the enunciation of the Monroe Doctrine in 1823. But the American government, in practice, was content with playing a lone hand. When the country went to war with Britain for the second time in 1812, it avoided any kind of understanding with Napoleon. Monroe ended by acting unilaterally in dealing with the threat to Latin America. And, as time went on, the isolationist point of view was more and more dominant. The country was preoccupied with its own affairs; it was facing westward, not eastward. It was growing rapidly; it was unthreatened and stronger every year; it had no need of allies. The extent of its insistence on plowing its own furrow is to be seen in the fact that there were distinguished Americans who, on isolationist grounds, even doubted the wisdom of participation in the International Red Cross, and in the action of the Senate in 1899 in ratifying the Hague Convention for the pacific settlement of international disputes there were reservations alluding to the traditional policy of the United States against foreign entanglements. True, in this long period dissentient voices were occasionally heard, especially in the period of European revolutions at the middle of the century. But it was more important that, year after year, the words of the Farewell Address were solemnly read to the Senate on each birthday of Washington as the unchallenged wisdom of the greatest of all Americans.

It is necessary to add, moreover, that during the first hundred odd years of this country's history, the isolationist point of view corresponded with the interests of the United States, with the realities of international intercourse, and even with American ideals. The country was engaged in the colossal task of developing a continent; and it was not until well on in the century that, from the standpoint of population or resources, it attained the status of a great power. Furthermore, it was still deeply divided by a sectional conflict which was only resolved in the fierce fires of the Civil War. And it was, during a great part of the period, receiving a host of immigrants and forging a new American nationality out of the millions who came from the Old World to the New. None of these facts might have been controlling if Europe itself had not, for the most part, been at peace. But from 1815 to 1914 there was, on the other side of the Atlantic, no general war such as engaged the passions of Americans in the earliest period of its national history. Was it not reasonable, even in conformity with American aspirations, that in this period the United States should devote itself to the development of its own strength, to its own conceptions of liberty and progress, to the building of a more fruitful social and economic order, rather than to the assertion of its place in the larger world, especially since it was in no wise threatened by what went on there?

But if, then, during this long epoch Europe was a continent apart, whose interests, in the words of the first President, were "only remotely connected" with our own, the same could not be said of Latin America. In that continent the young American nation early took an interest, an interest excited by the revolutionary movements which began there in 1810 and which led to the recognition of some of the new states in 1822. This recognition was followed within less than two years by the declaration known as the Monroe Doctrine. The circumstances surrounding the enunciation of the Doctrine may be briefly cited. While republicanism was triumphing in the New World, the politics of the Old World were running a different course. The Napoleonic Wars were followed by reaction, and the governments of the Continent—France, Austria, Prussia, and

Russia—banded together to repress revolution. Intervention in Naples in 1821, and in Spain in 1823, aroused fears of similar action across the seas, fears felt in London as well as in Washington. In August of 1823 the British Foreign Secretary, George Canning, approached Richard Rush, the American minister, with proposals for a joint declaration on the question of the rebellious Spanish-American colonies.

The proposal was transmitted to Washington, where its arrival coincided, in the broad sense of the term, with some rather disquieting declarations on the part of Tsar Alexander I. Rejecting the British proposal for immediate joint action, President Monroe laid down the policy of the United States in the famous message of December 2, 1823, in which he declared that any intervention on the part of the Old World powers "with the purpose of oppressing, or controlling in any other manner, the destiny of the new republics" would be "regarded as the manifestation of an unfriendly disposition towards the United States." The danger, we now know, was illusory; the Monroe administration, moreover, soon refused to translate its bold words into the more precise terms of an alliance with the states of Latin America; but a principle had been enunciated which was to be of immense influence in the future. And with this principle was coupled another. Seizing the occasion offered by a controversy with Russia over the northwest coast, Monroe, at the suggestion of Adams, declared that "the American continents, by the free and independent condition which they have assumed and maintain, are henceforth not to be considered as subject for future colonization by any European power."

The language of Monroe was by no means regarded from that very moment as decisively indicating a line of policy. But its popularity grew with time. In the forties the principle of the Doctrine was again asserted by President Polk, this time with regard to Oregon, with an eye to California and Texas as well and even to Central America and Yucatan. By the middle of the fifties the phrase "Monroe Doctrine" appears. And when, in the sixties, taking advantage of the Civil War, Emperor Napoleon III attempted to set up a monarchy in Mexico under an Austrian prince, Americans reacted vigorously. While Secretary Seward never mentioned the Doctrine by name in this connection, his assertion of its principle was an important contributing factor to the final collapse of the Mexican project, when the end of the Civil War freed the hands of the United States for action.

In the years which followed, the Doctrine tended to expand. Thus President Grant connected it with the idea that the United States could not see with indifference the transfer of New World territory from one European power to another. President Hayes attempted to connect it with American opposition to an interoceanic canal controlled by any European state. And President Cleveland went so far as to insist that in a controversy over boundaries between an American and European state, involving New World territory (specifically, a controversy between Venezuela and Great Britain over the limits of British Guiana), the United States had a right to insist upon the arbitration of the dispute. The great outburst of popular feeling which accompanied his action amply demonstrated how increasingly sensitive American opinion was to the principles originally affirmed by Monroe. Finally, to extend this summary a little beyond the end of the century, Theodore Roosevelt asserted that the Monroe Doctrine might compel the United States to exercise a kind of international police power in the New World against unruly states which would otherwise be threatened with the intervention of European powers.

In the latter part of the nineteenth century, the maxims we have just been examining began to be reinforced by a closer relationship between the United States and the states of Latin America. The first attempt at a Pan-American Congress came as early as 1826 and was largely a fiasco. The government at Washington was not represented in such meetings as that at Santiago in 1856 or at Lima in 1863. But in the 1880's James G. Blaine, a boldly imaginative Secretary of State, sought to bring about a conference of the New World states in Washington. The meeting was not actually held until 1889, but when it did come about it paved the way for the association of the cisatlantic republics in an organization which was to grow into an important agency of international cooperation, in the form of the Pan-American Union, and which led to further conferences of mounting importance in the course of the twentieth century.

The interest of the United States in Latin America was, as we shall have occasion to emphasize later, closely connected with the notion of American security. It has been often stated that this security interest was virtually guaranteed by the might of the British navy, and this assertion became particularly popular and widespread in the period just before American entry into the Second World War, when to many persons it seemed desirable to emphasize the coincidence of British and American interests. But the matter ought not to be put in exactly this way. As a matter of fact, most of the challenges to the Doctrine in the nineteenth century came from Great Britain: the occupation of the Falkland Islands (claimed by Argentina) in 1833, small expansions in Central America, the Bay Islands, British Honduras, and the so-called Mosquito Coast of Nicaragua, and (if one chooses to call it a challenge) the British attitude in the boundary controversy with Venezuela over the limits of British Guiana. On the other side of the account, it is fair to say that the London government usually retreated, at least in substantial degree, when confronted with American opposition. We need not exaggerate the services to the Doctrine performed by Britain, but neither should we fail to recognize that little damage was done to American interests by any of the enterprises mentioned above.

As for the other great nations of Europe, it was not British power but their own national interests that led them to keep their hands off Latin America. True, under Louis Napoleon, as we have just seen, the French did intervene in Mexico and set up a puppet monarchy under the Austrian Archduke Maximilian. But this enterprise collapsed, as much as a result of the gallant resistance of the Mexicans themselves, and the complications of European politics, as because of the hostility of the United States. After this time (1866–67), French energies were exerted in Africa and Asia. Tunis became a protectorate in 1881, and Morocco fell more and more under French control, becoming a protectorate in 1912. In southeastern Asia, starting with Cochin China in 1862, France gradually extended its influence over Cambodia, Laos, and Annam, consolidating its position there by 1884. Germany, like France, had other fish to fry than the Latin American variety. Its interests were centered in the Near East and in colonial expansion in Africa; even in the first years of the twentieth century, the German Foreign Office, despite the rise of German nationalism, took a cautious view of any expansion in the New World. Russia had the Balkans to think about, as well as its expansion towards the Pacific and in the areas peripheral to China. Moreover, its naval power was hardly such as to suggest ambitious enterprises across the Atlantic. Taking the situation as a whole, it is fair to say that the Monroe Doctrine owed its strength not to the material power of the United States—which, in terms of naval or military might, was far from considerable during most of the nineteenth century—but to a fortunate international situation.

Safe from any threat from abroad, the young republic could, then, devote itself to steady expansion across the continent. At the time of the peace treaty of 1783, the United States, if the line of settlement had been followed, might well have been confined for the most part to the region between the Appalachians and the Atlantic. But at the very outset of its history it was, in a sense, the child of fortune. For in the making of the terms of peace, largely through the indifference of the British to the wilderness area across the mountains and through their desire to win back at least a part of the loyalty and friendship which they had lost, the new nation was endowed with a very substantial territorial area, extending from the Atlantic to the Mississippi and from the Great Lakes to the thirty-first parallel.

A second stroke of fortune followed within twenty years. West of the Mississippi, at the end of the eighteenth century, there extended a vast area loosely known as Louisiana, then in the hands of Spain. In a temporary burst of colonial ambition, Napoleon Bonaparte secured this section from the decaying monarchy of the Iberian peninsula in 1800; then, wearying of the role which he had temporarily assumed and faced with the possibility of a new war with Britain, he transferred it to the United States, for the small sum of fifteen million dollars. By this single transaction the territory under the control of the American government was more than doubled.

On the southern borders of the United States east of the Mississippi, there still remained the Spanish border province of Florida. But the western part of this province was soon settled by American frontiersmen; in 1810 a revolution against Spanish rule broke out there; and, claiming to be acting under the terms of the Louisiana treaty of cession (which were, indeed, comfortably ambiguous), President Madison ordered this part to be occupied. For a while Spanish rule in East Florida remained; but the hold of the court of Madrid upon this province was a tenuous one, and by 1819 the Spaniards, convinced that they must make the best of a bad business, negotiated a treaty of cession with the United States.

For a time American expansion was now arrested; but before very long the process that had taken place in West Florida was repeated, in somewhat different terms, with regard to Texas. There, too, the frontiersmen moved into territory somewhat sparsely occupied; there, too, the hold of Mexico, the successor of Spain, was shaken by revolution; and revolution, after a decent interval, was followed by the territory's annexation to the United States, or rather by the admission of the independent state of Texas into the Union.

The Mexicans were loath to recognize the incorporation of erstwhile Mexican territory into the United States. The Texan question was one of the principal causes of the war which broke out between the American and Mexican peoples in 1846, and the American victory in that war resulted in a new enlargement of the national domain. California and parts of Arizona, New Mexico, Nevada, and Utah were now added to the territorial area of the American government.

In the same period, the forties, the frontiers of the United States in the north were made more precise. The Webster-Ashburton Treaty of 1842 finally settled the disputed boundary between Maine and British Canada (insofar as it had not been previously fixed); and by the same compact an important area in Minnesota, the seat of the important Mesabi iron deposits, was added to the national domain. Further west, Great Britain and the United States had for more than twenty years, by agreement, left the Oregon country free and open to the citizens of both nations; but by a treaty of 1846, the forty-ninth parallel was recognized as the boundary, and the territory south of this line, with the exception of Vancouver Island, became a part of the young republic.

The final act in the rounding out of the territory of the United States was the Gadsden Purchase of 1853, which added a small region in the southwest, necessary to the building of a transcontinental railroad line. But the purchase of Alaska from Russia in 1867 brought within American jurisdiction another vast expanse of territory, the value of which could hardly be suspected at the time and which, of course, was still within the continental area of North America.

In contemplating the process which has just been described, Americans have usually been quite well satisfied with the bases of their own action; and it is the case that in only one instance did the enlargement of the territorial area of the United States come about through a war. Yet it may be worth while to observe that a severe moralist could find grounds on which to criticize American policy; in 1803, for example, the American government purchased Louisiana from Napoleon, even though the Emperor had promised the Spaniards that he would not alienate it and had violated the French constitution in so doing; the acquisition of West Florida was brought about, as we have said, by a revolution, one which President Madison certainly did nothing to discourage and of which he promptly took advantage; the cession of East Florida in 1819 was undoubtedly accelerated by the heavy-handed action of General Andrew Jackson, who, in 1818, acting on his own authority, occupied a large part of the province. In the Texan revolution, the American government acted with formal correctness; but aid for the movement came from the United States nonetheless. Of the responsibility for the Mexican War, we shall have more to say later; but it can be stated here that reproaches have often been directed at the Polk administration for its conduct in connection with the conflict. As for the Gadsden Purchase, though wearing the appearance of a voluntary cession, there are aspects of the whole transaction that seem rather shoddy when analyzed in detail.

Yet the moralistic judgment with regard to great events has a somewhat limited validity; it is possible to regard the expansion of the United States as a kind of biological process which could hardly have been arrested and which was carried on with less violence than often goes with such activities. It is necessary, moreover, to emphasize one important point. The territory acquired by the United States in the rounding out of the national domain was assimilated to the original area, that is, was endowed with the institutions of self-government and constituted into states which were admitted into the Union. American expansion, in other words, involved none of those vexing problems that have so often followed in the wake of European wars of conquest. There were no resentful minorities, in important numbers, to whom American rule was obnoxious. There were no acute problems of assimilation. An immensely strong nation was the result.

The rounding out of the continental domain of the United States was completed, as we have seen, by 1853, or, if one includes Alaska, by 1867; there were, before the end of this period, signs of an interest in regions beyond our borders. For example, as early as the third decade of the century, American missionaries had established themselves in Hawaii and were exercising a very considerable influence upon the rather rudimentary royal government. In 1842 Daniel Webster sounded a warning against the interference of other powers in the affairs of the island, and, in 1853, a treaty of annexation was actually negotiated, though it was never ratified by the Senate. Twenty-five years later, a reciprocity treaty tied the Hawaiian economy securely to that of the United States. In the seventies, too, the American government began to display an interest in Samoa, and in 1889 it entered into a kind of condominium for the government of the islands with Great Britain and Germany. And often throughout the period, as early as the 1820's, with increasing stridency in the fifties, and again in the period 1868 to 1878, there were voices raised in favor of the acquisition of Cuba. On the other hand, the country rejected the plans of Seward for the acquisition of the Danish West Indies in 1867 and a presentation by the Grant administration of a treaty proposing annexation of the Dominican Republic. In the nineties, however, decisive events occurred. The Cuban revolt of 1895 aroused American opinion deeply, and that opinion was the more inflamed because two great newspaper lords in New York, Joseph Pulitzer and William Randolph Hearst, were engaged in a fierce journalistic competition that led them to adopt every possible sensational device to dramatize the Cuban struggle for independence. The sentiment for intervention in the conflict was powerful even at the outset of the McKinley administration; but it rose to fever heat after the sinking (no man knows by whom) of the battleship *Maine* in Havana harbor in the winter of 1898. The President and his advisers found themselves swept on towards war; and, though the weak government of Spain was willing to make large concessions to prevent a clash of arms, the clash came.

The nation that emerged from the war of 1898 was not the nation which had entered it. Though the war had been fought for the liberation of Cuba, it ended with the acquisition of Puerto Rico, Guam, and the Philippines, and with a new sense of national power. Under Theodore Roosevelt, who succeeded to the presidency on the death of President McKinley in 1901, the nation began to play a more active role than ever before in world affairs, and the buoyant self-confidence of the national leader both reflected and was reflected in the temper of the people at large. A new era had begun, an era which extends to our own time.

In dealing with this new era, let us first examine American policy in the Orient. As we have already seen, the United States had manifested an interest in Hawaii and Samoa even before the Spanish-American War. This interest was now intensified; during the conflict itself Hawaii was annexed, and shortly thereafter, by an agreement with Germany and Great Britain, a part of the Samoan islands came into American hands.

Not long after came a new concern with the affairs of China. Perhaps this interest stemmed from somewhat romantic ideas as to the vast market that the Middle Kingdom offered to the trade of the West; it was also connected with the influence of American missionaries. In obedience to it, John Hay, McKinley's Secretary of State, tried to commit the powers to freedom of commercial opportunity in China and to respect for the territorial integrity of this great state. It cannot truly be said that he succeeded; but the principles that he laid down (the principles of the Open Door, as they became known) were accepted by American public opinion and were destined to have an immense influence on the future. Still another sign of a more active policy was to be found in the fact that, when the Boxer Rebellion broke out and a wave of antiforeignism swept China, President McKinley sent American troops to march beside those of the European powers to the relief of the besieged legations in Peking.

Only a few years later a new phase of our relations began with Japan. It was the American government which, by a judicious mixture of persuasion and veiled force, had opened the island empire to the trade of the world in the decade of the fifties. During the rest of the nineteenth century the relations of Washington and Tokyo had been almost uniformly friendly. Friendly they still were at the outbreak of the Russo-Japanese War in 1904, but soon a new element of tension appeared. President Roosevelt's good offices at the end of the war, which culminated in the Peace of Portsmouth, seemed to many Japanese to have deprived them of the fruits of victory; and the segregation of Japanese school children in San Francisco produced a substantial tension between the two governments, which was allayed only by the brilliant diplomacy of the President. More fundamental was the stimulus to Japanese ambitions offered by the outbreak of the world war in Europe; it was not strange, perhaps, international politics being what they are, that the Japanese attempted to make hay while the sun shone. At the very outset of the struggle, they seized the German-held port of Kiaochow; in 1915 they formulated a series of demands on China which, if accepted as they stood, would have transformed that nation into a Japanese protectorate. Before the armistice of 1918 they had thrown a substantial force into Siberia, on the pretext of protecting that region against the Bolsheviks. And they had proceeded to embark upon a great naval program as well. The United States was in no position to hamper the Japanese program, while engaged in a great struggle in Europe; and at Versailles Woodrow Wilson, although with the utmost reluctance, was compelled to acquiesce in the transfer of Germany's economic rights in Shantung to Japan. His decision was bitterly denounced by his partisan enemies at home; the prospects of a naval competition loomed large; and the tension between Tokyo and Washington was considerable when the Republican administration of President Harding took office in March 1921.

For a time the statesmanship of conciliation was equal to the occasion. The famous Washington Conference of 1921–22 was a remarkable effort to bring about a constructive settlement of the many problems of the Orient. In the field of naval limitation a treaty was signed fixing ratios for the great powers in capital ships and airplane carriers, and the assent of the Japanese to a position inferior to that of the United States was secured by a promise on our part not to fortify Guam or the Philippines. At the same time, in the Nine-Power Treaty, the principles of the Hay notes were now embodied in a formal diplomatic instrument. By these agreements, it was hoped that the government at Tokyo, freed from any physical menace on the part of the United States, could be persuaded to pursue a moderate and statesmanlike policy. The American government, in a gesture of faith, virtually divested itself of physical power in the Far East in the belief that its abdication would pave the way for moderate and peaceful policies on the part of its rival.

At first this belief seemed likely to be confirmed. The decade of the twenties was, on the whole, one of good relations between the United States and Japan. The principal disturbance, indeed, came from the action of the American Congress in 1924 in proscribing Japanese immigration into the United States, instead of permitting a trifling number of the Japanese to come in under a quota system. The affront to Japanese pride was profound, but it did not prevent the powers from continuing to pursue a conciliatory policy, and, in 1930, at the London Conference, the Japanese put their signatures to a remarkable treaty of naval disarmament which fixed quotas for all types of ships.

The coming of the Great Depression, however, profoundly affected the situation in the Far East, paving the way for the rise of Japanese militarism to power. The naval treaty was violently condemned in Japan; it was ratified only with extreme difficulty, and after shameful political assassinations. And, in 1931, in defiance of their own foreign office, the Japanese militarists proceeded to take possession of the province of Manchuria, in which up to that time Japan had only strictly qualified rights. The reaction of the Hoover administration was immediate; an attempt was made to bring pressure to bear upon Tokyo through the instrumentality of the League of Nations and through the so-called Kellogg-Briand Pact, which bound the signatory nations not to resort to war as an instrument of national policy; but it was clear from the beginning that, on the one hand, nothing but force could restrain the Japanese and, on the other, that the American administration had no willingness to press beyond the field of exhortation and moral pressure. This may not have been true of Secretary of State Henry L. Stimson, but it was certainly true of the President and perhaps of majority public opinion. It is difficult to see how American action did aught but exacerbate a far-from-easy situation.

More and more, as time went on, the Japanese militarists came to control the situation. More and more the Japanese put forward ambitious pretensions to the overlordship of the Far East. The Roosevelt administration may well at the beginning of its term of office have hoped to let matters quiet down; but there was no intention to act on this basis in Tokyo. At the end of 1934 the naval treaties of Washington and London were denounced; the Japanese proceeded to expand their forces and, on the economic side, to strengthen their grip on the territories gained from China. In 1937 they began an actual war with the government of Chiang Kai-shek, a war which aimed at nothing less than the control of the Middle Kingdom.

It was natural that American opinion should react against this unabashed imperialism. Roosevelt had been very cautious in his utterances on international affairs during his first term; but, in October of 1937, he ventured for the first time to express the opinion that lawbreaking nations should be placed in quarantine. His speech found little response at the time, but as Japanese purposes in China became clearer and clearer, the administration moved, and was moved, toward positive action. At the end of 1938 it made the first of a series of loans to China, and, in the summer of 1939, it denounced its commercial treaty with Japan. In the same period there began a substantial naval expansion that could hardly fail to produce its reaction in the island empire. In the meantime the Japanese militarists secured an increasing ascendancy over the policy of their government. The victories of Germany in the spring of 1940 and the occupation of France were followed in due course by a Japanese alliance with the Axis. While, on the one hand, the ambitions of Nippon expanded, on the other, American assistance to China, and American determination not to recognize Japanese conquests there, increased the tension between the two governments. The Japanese occupation of southern Indochina in the summer of 1941 produced a severance of trade relations by the United States. Futile negotiations, futile because neither side would surrender on the Chinese question, were followed by the attack on Pearl Harbor in December 1941.

The growth of American interests in the Orient might, in theory, have run a different course. A distinguished American historian, Samuel F. Bemis, describes the acquisition of the Philippines as the great aberration; and the material gains that sprang from this departure from the past were no doubt incommensurate with the sacrifices involved in playing a large role in the Far East, with greatly increased problems of national defense, and with the heavy involvements of the years to follow. But again, as in the case of American expansion, we are dealing with process rather than with principle; with the urge of a great nation to enlarge its sphere of influence and of activity. The page has been written and cannot be recalled; and once the conquest of the American continent had been completed, it was natural, perhaps (if the word has any meaning) inevitable, that the American people should begin to look beyond their borders and seek to play a greater part on the stage of the world.

Let us turn from the story of American action in the Orient to the relations of the United States with Europe.

We have already examined the foundations of American isolationism and seen how deep were its roots. There was a brief departure from the traditional viewpoint in the administration of Theodore Roosevelt, when the United States participated in the conference of Algeciras, called to solve the problem of Franco-German rivalry with regard to the kingdom of Morocco, and when, indeed, in advance of the conference the President used his influence in behalf of conciliation and peace. But in the face of rising tension in Europe, the Taft administration pursued a policy of aloofness. When the First World War broke out in 1914, the first reaction of the great body of Americans was, no doubt, in favor of neutrality, and the Wilson administration reflected this feeling. But an objective judgment of the events of the period that followed soon proved to be impossible, either to the man in the street or to the man in the White House. The war, like the great conflicts of the French Revolution, inevitably aroused, and to some extent divided, public sentiment. The weight of opinion was, however, on the side of the Allies. And this was certainly true of the President himself. Though, in theory, Wilson sought to follow an impartial course, in private he early gave expression to his apprehension of a German victory. American policy was tipped in favor of the enemies of Germany. The early violations of international law by Great Britain were made the subject of formal protests, protests too obviously halfhearted to effect any substantial change in British policy. But, when the Germans in the winter of 1915 initiated submarine warfare against merchant vessels (a step, it is true, unprecedented and, therefore, in 1915 particularly shocking), the administration from the first adopted an attitude of sharp condemnation. It stood on the right of Americans to travel not only on American but on belligerent merchant vessels. And after the sinking of the British liner *Lusitania,* with the loss of over a hundred American lives, any retreat from this position was almost impossible.

Mindful of the gravity of the issue, the President adopted no bellicose course at this time. He sought by diplomatic means to bring the Germans to an abandonment of the U-boat war, and in 1916 he succeeded. That the country appreciated these efforts, that large elements of opinion desired, if possible, to keep out of the European conflict, was demonstrated by the great vote for Wilson, especially in the Middle West, the area most opposed to involvement, in the election of 1916. It is, indeed, difficult to see on what issue the United States would have entered the war had the government at Berlin continued to abstain from the use of the submarine. But the Germans chose a different course, and the resumption of the underseas activities led first to a breach of relations and then to war.

The entry of the United States into the First World War marks an epoch in the history of American foreign policy. For the first time American soldiers crossed the broad Atlantic to take part in a conflict on European soil and cast their decisive weight into the scales. The momentous character of the decision is indicated by the change which took place in Woodrow Wilson himself. In his public utterances he had at times affected to believe that no great differences in moral outlook separated the Allies and the Central Powers. In his famous "peace without victory" address of January 22, 1917, something of this attitude remained. But in his war address of April 6, 1917, Wilson made the central issue of the war a struggle to destroy autocracy and to establish an international organization for the maintenance of peace through collective action of the nations against an aggressor. Because the establishment of such an organization would be promising for the future only if the terms of settlement at the end of the war were such as seemed reasonable and just, the President found himself involved in the specifics of peacemaking, no less than in the general elements of the problem, and with high conscience he went to Paris, after the victory of 1918, in an effort to see to it that his ideals, so loftily promulgated during the war, were recognized and embodied in the engagements of Versailles. No one who studies the story of his diplomacy there in detail can doubt the integrity of his purpose, or fail to see that in some important respects he was successful.

But it is almost inevitable that a mood of disillusionment should, in some degree, follow a period of war. Obviously, when victory was won, the interests of the Allied powers were bound to diverge. And, obviously, compromises were the only means of reconciling them. It is not possible here to analyze the peace settlements in detail. Inevitably, however, to many unsophisticated Americans, unaccustomed to judging the questions of international politics on a realistic basis, they bore the aspect of a series of sordid deals or unworthy concessions. Moreover, wholly apart from any generalized view, there were many groups in America bound to react against the Treaty of Versailles. German-Americans thought it unduly severe; Italo-Americans disliked Wilson's unyielding refusal to concede the port of Fiume to Italy; Irish-Americans reacted against the close association with Britain that had come about in the war; and American traditionalists were not ready to abandon the principle of nonentanglement to take part in a world organization which might commit the United States to positive action for the preservation of peace. The Senate of 1919, controlled by the Republican opponents of the President, insisted upon reservations to the treaty. The President refused to accept such reservations, and the issue was, most unwisely, thrown into the campaign of 1920. There the pro-League candidate suffered a resounding defeat, and the Republican President, Warren G. Harding, rejected all association with the League.

In the period of the twenties American policy was a curious compound of international cooperation and isolationism. In such agreements as the Washington Treaty, the United States played a great part in bringing about international understanding. Though it had not ratified the Treaty of Versailles, it was not averse to assisting in the settlement of the question of German reparations, and was responsible in no small degree for the temporarily workable arrangements known as the Dawes Plan (1924) and the Young Plan (1929). American administrations urged American adhesion to the protocol creating the Court of International Justice. Towards the end of the period Americans were participating in many of the League's activities. In 1928, in a gesture which, if not particularly effective, was an expression of American idealism, the United States promoted the Kellogg Pact. But in this same period the United States closed the door to immigration, insisted upon the payment (though not the total payment) of the debts owed to it by its Allies, while at the same time raising its tariff wall to make such payments impossible, and studiously avoided any commitment to help keep the peace by economic or other action.

The years that immediately followed the Great Depression did nothing to strengthen the spirit of international cooperation in the United States. On the contrary, they were marked by a strong revulsion against the involvement in European affairs. The legend grew up that we had been swept into the world war by incompetent leadership, by the pressure of financial interests, by the subtle propaganda of the Allies. In order to prevent the same thing from happening again, Congress enacted and President Roosevelt signed what was described as neutrality legislation: legislation forbidding travel on belligerent merchant ships, forbidding loans to belligerents, forbidding traffic in arms and ammunition, and insisting that all other purchases be paid for before being sent outside the bounds of the United States. There was a certain persuasive quality in the reasoning on which this legislation was based. Loans there had been, trade there had been, propaganda there had been twenty years before; it was easy to make these the central explanation of 1917, and to fail to see how difficult it was to establish a nexus between any of them and the actual policy of the Wilson administration, to fail, too, to recognize the possible fact that in helping to make German defeat certain the United States was serving its own interests in the period of the First World War.

By 1939, however, the aggressions of Hitler had produced an immense change in American opinion. There was a deeper realization of the danger of American involvement; there was a more united sentiment against the Germans; there was a more widespread feeling that the victory of the Reich might involve a genuine peril to the United States. President Roosevelt reflected and stimulated this point of view. As early as the fall of 1939, he called for and obtained the repeal of the arms embargo which hampered the action of the democratic nations. With the fall of France (which administered a severe shock to the complacent) he courageously declared for assistance to the democracies. The country echoed his mood. The Republican nomination of Wendell Willkie, an avowed friend of positive aid, the adoption of a conscription law in time of peace without any special pressure from the White House, indicated the national temper. The President himself proved a resolute and imaginative leader, sometimes moving in advance of the people, sometimes merely interpreting their desires, but always clear as to his own and the nation's ultimate purpose. In the fall of 1940 came a bargain by which Britain was given fifty destroyers in exchange for the right conceded to the United States to fortify various British-held posts, ranging from Newfoundland to Trinidad. In the winter of 1941, Congress passed the famous measure known as Lend-Lease, by which the United States put its immense material power behind Britain. Bit by bit, thereafter, the American government expanded its activities in protection of the cargoes it was sending abroad, occupying Greenland in April and Iceland in July of 1940, extending its patrols and finally resorting to convoy in the North Atlantic; in September the President directed the shooting of German submarines on sight; in November he called for the arming of American merchant ships and free navigation of the waters around Great Britain. It is difficult to see how, in any case, war could have been avoided for very long; but the question was settled, when after Pearl Harbor, in obedience to the terms of a treaty of alliance signed in September 1940, Hitler and Mussolini declared war on the United States. In Europe, as in the Orient, a new epoch was opening in the foreign policy of the United States.

The evolution of American diplomacy in the first half of the twentieth century from isolationism to involvement in the affairs of Europe corresponds, as may already have been suggested, with a great change in the European scene itself and with the shifting of the balance of power. Great Britain, in her long ascendancy in world affairs, never

threatened the safety or the peace of the American continents. Whether Wilhelminian Germany, had it been victorious in the war of 1914-1918, would have done so is a
question which cannot be answered definitively (though it
is fair to say that not a few Americans in the years of the
First World War would have answered it in the affirmative). But of the danger in the forties there can be little
doubt. The victory of Hitler, especially a victory followed,
as it might well have been, by a vast expansion of military
power and by new and destructive weapons of warfare in
the hands of a psychopath, would have been a disaster. But
the defeat of Hitler did not bring about a world in which
the United States could return to isolationism. The ambition and the aspirations of the Soviet Union soon were seen
to present a new danger. The place of the United States in
the world at large was challenged as it had never been challenged before. That there should be an immense alteration
in the American mood was a foregone conclusion, especially since the material strength of the nation was now
adequate to the assumption of great international responsibilities. Of what followed I shall have more to say in a
succeeding chapter.

In this introductory chapter, I intend to deal more cur-
sorily with inter-American relations. The imperialism which
prompted the acquisition of the Philippines was not absent
from United States policy towards the states of the New
World. But the quality, extent, and significance of this imperialism deserve separate consideration elsewhere. In the
main, I call attention here simply to the growth in the
strength of the Pan-American ideal. At the beginning of
the century there was still only the loosest association of
American states. In the First World War, the largest of
these states, with one exception, Brazil, were all of them

neutral—Mexico, Chile, Argentina, Venezuela, Colombia. But the years of the thirties saw a great change, one full of meaning for the future. In 1936, for example, the American states agreed to consult together against the possibility of aggression from the Old World. In 1938, at the Conference of Lima, they implemented this decision by a protocol which called for a meeting of the foreign ministers of the republics on the call of any one of them. In 1939, they concerted measures of financial and economic assistance at the Congress of Panama. In 1940, at Havana, they went on record as declaring that an act of aggression against any one of them would be considered an act of aggression against all, and they provided the machinery for the taking over of European colonies in the New World, if these colonies were threatened by the action of the aggressor. In 1942, they went on record in favor of a rupture of relations with the Axis. True, these measures were not all received with unanimous enthusiasm. In particular, the government of the Argentine manifested an obstructionist and jealous attitude. But, on the whole, the amazing thing was the growth of the spirit of Pan-American solidarity. In this, as in other areas, the position of the United States at the close of the period was one of far greater strength and influence than at the beginning. Here, for the present, we may leave this summary story of American diplomacy and turn to an examination of some of the central questions which the historian of trends and ideas may wish to ask with regard to the foreign policy of the United States.

II

Is There an American Imperialism?

<hr/>

IT is a truism, but one that needs to be constantly reiterated, that words are often used by men to arouse emotion and fortify prejudice, rather than to describe exactly
or appeal to reason. The language of politics, national and
international, is full of clichés which serve these convenient
purposes. To many of those who lean towards the left, the
partisans of the right are always "reactionaries"; while no
other word than "radical" or "socialist" or perhaps "Communist" will satisfy some conservatives in describing the
friends of moderate change. In international affairs,
"honor" and "justice" and the "interests of humanity" are
likely to be the exclusive concern of one nation, while sinister motives are unvaryingly ascribed to its rival, together
with what is usually described since the days of Hitler as
"warmongering." Among the convenient terms of abuse in
the vocabulary of contemporary international politics is
the term "imperialism." To the Soviet Union the peoples of
the West and, particularly, the United States are imperialists. The cliché has wide influence; beyond question, along
with many other Russian propaganda devices, it produces
a certain degree of confusion in the minds of excellent people who are not free from a touch of masochism; and it

reminds the newborn nations of the world of the "oppression" which preceded their liberation. It is well worth while, then, to examine what is termed American imperialism, to determine its character and its limitations, and to assess the strength of the imperialist motive in American foreign policy historically and in the present day.

At the outset of this analysis it is important to draw a clear distinction between expansion and imperialism. Expansion, in the view that will be taken in the following pages, is the process by which the political control of a given nation is extended over territory which then becomes assimilated and incorporated in the political and constitutional system of the expanding state. The cession of Louisiana by France to the United States in 1803, or even the acquisition of California by conquest from Mexico in 1848, are examples of expansion. The regions thus acquired became a part of the federal union, and whatever moral judgment we may wish to make with regard to these acquisitions, we shall naturally recognize the fact that today the regions so acquired present no special problem, so far as their political status is concerned, but constitute parts of a united nation.

The question of how to deal with territories acquired outside the continental area of the United States did not arise until the end of the nineteenth century. Not that there was no appetite for such territories. Americans had had their eyes on Cuba since the days of Jefferson; on at least two occasions the purchase of the island was seriously discussed, and once, in the case of the well-known Ostend Manifesto, its seizure, in the event that Spain refused to sell, was somewhat blatantly advocated. After the Mexican War there was a movement for the annexation of all of Mexico, and in 1848 President Polk proposed the occupation of Yucatan. Just after the Civil War Secretary Seward negotiated a treaty for the purchase of the Danish West Indies; and President Grant proposed the annexation of the Dominican Republic. But none of these projects came to fruition. Down to 1860 Northern antagonism to slavery put a damper on the acquisition of any territory which might increase the influence of the South; and in the twenty years after the Civil War the country was primarily concerned with the problems of reconstruction and with its own remarkable internal development. In the period of the Spanish-American War, however, as we have already seen, the United States acquired dominion over Puerto Rico, Guam, and the Philippines, and in 1899 it acquired title to a part of the Samoan islands. In 1903, taking advantage of the revolution which gave birth to the independent republic of Panama, the American government established a virtual protectorate over the new state and secured the Panama Canal Zone. In 1916 it bought the Virgin Islands. And in the twenty-year period between 1898 and 1918, it intervened in the affairs of Cuba for a brief period (1906–1909) and occupied for longer intervals the territory of three independent states, Nicaragua, Haiti, and the Dominican Republic. It would seem reasonable to describe this period as one of American imperialism, and it is well worth while to examine what this "imperialism" was like in practice.

There is one essential generalization with which we ought to begin. American rule over other peoples has always been rule with an uneasy conscience. Implicit in it at all times has been faith in the democratic process, the belief that it was the duty of an imperial power to prepare the way to self-government for the peoples over whom it exercised control. This is something that ought never to be forgotten in any discussion of the whole problem. Indeed, it means that "imperialism," as it is conceived by the Americans, can be only a passing phase. We can see this principle at work in the discussions at the end of the Spanish-American War. The very assumption of imperial rule over the territories acquired from Spain was bitterly contested in principle. The idea of such rule was regarded by substantial numbers of Americans—including some eminent members of the dominant Republican Party—as inconsistent with the Declaration of Independence and the Constitution. The treaty for the acquisition of these territories passed the Senate with a single vote to spare, after vigorous congressional and public debate and, although the imperialists won, the anti-imperialists, in a sense, called the tune. The establishment of a wide measure of self-government for the peoples brought under American sway was regarded as desirable by both parties and became the basis of American policy. Let us look at the record in this respect, first of all in the case of the Philippines.

After a brief period of military rule and the unsavory episode of American repression of a Filipino insurrection, a civil government was established in the islands in 1901, and the Filipinos were admitted to not a few administrative offices. By 1907 a Filipino Assembly had been created, with complete legislative power, a commissioner elected to the United States House of Representatives to watch over the interests of the islands, and a majority of Filipinos established on the Filipino Commission, which carried on the work of the administration under the direction of the governor and which also exercised legislative powers. In 1916 a two-chamber legislature was created and, though the right of veto existed in the governor, under the Wilson administration wide authority was given to the new body, and it was left free to formulate general policies with little interference. There was a reaction under the governorship of General Leonard Wood, who displayed a somewhat autocratic temper, but this was short-lived. Finally, in 1934, Congress provided for the calling of a constitutional convention and for the complete independence of the islands. There was to be an interim period during which the United States was represented in the islands by a high commissioner, with strictly limited powers; but this lasted for only ten years, and in 1946 the independent Filipino Republic came into being. While the United States, with the consent of the Filipino government, retains bases in the islands, it no longer exercises any direct political authority over the conduct of Filipino affairs.

Let us look next at Puerto Rico. For a short time the island remained under military government. But in 1900 there was set up a civil regime which provided for a legislature, the lower house of which was elected by the Puerto Ricans themselves, and which gave to the island a civil governor. This very moderate measure of popular control was enlarged by the Jones Act of 1917. By this legislation, both houses of the Puerto Rican legislature were to be chosen by the inhabitants of the island, a substantial number of the administrative posts were placed in their hands, a bill of rights was enacted, and a Puerto Rican commissioner was given a seat in the House of Representatives. Thus the way was provided for a greater degree of self-rule. In 1947, still another step was taken. The governor of the island, instead of being chosen by the President of the United States, was henceforth to be elected by the Puerto Ricans and was to hold office for a fixed term. Virtually the whole administrative machinery was placed in native hands, leaving only the judges of the supreme court to be chosen by the President of the United States. And while, in theory, the power of veto over Puerto Rican legislation exists, and can be exercised either by the President or through congressional enactment, in practice the inhabitants of the island enjoy a wide degree of self-government.

The other territories acquired by the United States are Samoa, Guam, and the Virgin Islands, all of them small ones, with populations in each case under 60,000. The first two have been under naval rule, but even here there has been some representation accorded to the native population, and Guam has been transferred to civil authority. The third enjoys today the status accorded to Puerto Rico before the legislation of 1947. Even in these instances, then, the principle of self-government has been given expression.

In addition to controlling the territories mentioned, the United States exercised supervision and control over various Caribbean republics, setting up governments there which, in one form or another, were under the control of the American marines. Though a variety of motives explain these interventions (and we shall have more to say of this later), among them was the hope of bringing about orderly government based on a respect for constitutional and democratic processes. It may be instructive to see how much success was achieved. Indeed, by an analysis of the situation in these communities today, we may gain some insight into the fundamental question as to whether democratic institutions can be exported successfully and made to function efficiently.

The situation has varied in the five states under review (Panama, Cuba, Haiti, the Dominican Republic, and Nicaragua). In the Dominican Republic, for example, the departure of the Americans was soon followed by the establishment of a military dictatorship which was one of the most ruthless and cruel in the history of the Caribbean.

Rafael Leonidas Trujillo, until his death in 1961, governed the state with a rod of iron for more than thirty years. He certainly brought peace to the Dominicans, but to speak of democracy is out of the question. A somewhat milder autocratic rule was that established by Anastasio Somoza in Nicaragua. In Haiti, there have been better and worse rulers since American evacuation in 1934, but hardly popular government. In Cuba, there have also been better and worse periods. Interspersed with administrations which observed, to a substantial extent, democratic forms, there have been the dictatorships of Gerardo Machado, Fulgencio Batista, and Fidel Castro. The hope for genuine democracy in Cuba has never seemed less bright than it does as these words are written. Furthermore, even in the better eras, the venality and corruption of Cuban politicians has been notorious. The most hopeful picture presented has been that of Panama. There popular processes have been reasonably democratic. Yet there were revolutions in Panama in 1949 and 1951, and rule by a virtual dictator from 1951 to 1955.

As we look at the record as a whole we shall find in it some reason for questioning the universal validity of the democratic idea. We may well ask whether popular institutions are adapted to peoples with a very different tradition and a very different social composition from our own. We may well ask whether something does not depend upon political habit, whether something does not depend upon the diffusion of knowledge, whether something does not depend upon the existence of a broadly based middle class which desires order and peace and which, from its very position, practices those arts of compromise which are of the essence of democratic rule. The story of American interventions demonstrates that the imposition of a brief period of tutelage by no means guarantees the solidity of popular government, as we understand it in this country.

Whether one accepts these conclusions or not, however, the experiment carried on in the second two decades of the century was short-lived. With relation to Latin America, there has been a strong current of feeling that conducts the United States in a very different direction, and that was manifest even in the palmy days of the imperialist idea. In the period between 1910 and 1917, Mexico was in chronic disorder. The temptation to teach the Mexicans a lesson, to "clean up" a bad situation, was most certainly present. Yet neither the Taft nor the Wilson administration attempted to do anything of the kind. In the broad sense they let the Mexican peoples decide their own destinies. Wilson, it is true, found himself led by his prejudice against the Mexican dictator Victoriano Huerta to the occupation of Vera Cruz, a step which resulted in Huerta's overthrow, but he never desired full-scale intervention in Mexico. Even when the end of the war in Europe freed American hands from foreign complications, there was no attempt to police Mexico into good democratic behavior. The restraint shown by the United States was a remarkable example of the strength of the anti-imperialist impulse in American politics at a time when there was substantial pressure for another course of action. Policing little nations, rather than comparatively big ones, was as far as the United States was ready to go even in the imperialist decades.

Moreover, government by marines, inaugurated in Nicaragua in 1912, in the Dominican Republic in 1915, and in Haiti in 1916, did not long prove to be very popular with the American people. As early as the campaign of 1920, Senator Warren G. Harding, then a candidate for the presidency, actuated (it is fair to assume) by political motives rather than by profound knowledge of the situation in the Caribbean, sharply criticized the acts of the previous administration. And, with the advent of the Republican regime into power, the first steps were taken towards the liquidation of one of these military governments, that of the Dominican Republic, and the evacuation of Dominican territory was consummated in 1925. In the same year an attempt was made at withdrawal from Nicaragua and, though unsettled conditions again brought about American intervention, the way was soon prepared for a new withdrawal. In the meantime, important modifications were taking place in the view held by the United States with regard to the Roosevelt corollary of the Monroe Doctrine, which, as we have seen, formed a justification of interference in the affairs of other states. The State Department at this time (1928) drew up the famous Clark memorandum which, after analyzing the history of the Doctrine, came to the conclusion that it did not justify the use of force for the chastisement of unruly republics and the setting up of military rule. The next year the Senate of the United States, in ratifying the Kellogg-Briand Pact for the outlawry of war, adopted a kind of declaration or gloss on that instrument as to the limits to be placed on the principles of Monroe. At the time the Clark memorandum had not yet been published. Thus the Senate vote of 1929 was the first public repudiation by a body that was a part of the treaty-making power of the doctrine of intervention which had been practiced scarcely more than a decade before.

The change in American opinion was accelerated by the pressure of the Latin American republics themselves. At the Pan-American conference in Havana in 1928, the American delegation was made aware of the intensely critical attitude of most of our southern neighbors with regard to the whole problem of intervention. The administration, indeed, foreseeing what would be the tone of discussion there, had drawn Charles Evans Hughes from retirement to justify the position of the United States. But Hughes, though he was successful in postponing a vote on a resolution condemning all interventions, could not exorcise the essential hostility of the Latin American republics to the claims of the United States to exercise international police power. And the net result of the conference was probably to strengthen the movement away from imperialism.

It seems probable that the Great Depression also accentuated this tendency. The nation was in no mood, with the advent of the thirties, to use its physical power to protect American investors abroad. The hostility of the New Deal to the great financial interests made it relatively easy for the Roosevelt administration to forswear the habits of the past and place our relationship with Latin America on a new basis. At the Conference of Montevideo in 1933, Secretary Hull put his name to a protocol which bound the signatory states to abstain from all interference in the domestic concerns of any one of them. True, the Secretary boggled slightly at the proposed formula, and he even made a reservation intended to leave the door open for positive action for the protection of American interests. But the Senate of the United States, amazingly enough, ratified this protocol unanimously, and in 1936, when at Buenos Aires a new declaration was drawn up asserting the same principle in stronger terms, it was accepted without difficulty by the American delegation and ratified, like its predecessor, without a dissenting vote in the Senate.

In 1948 the United States went further. At the Conference of Bogota it put its name to a protocol which declared: "no state or *group of states* has the right to intervene, directly or indirectly, in the internal or external affairs of any other state. The foregoing principle prohibits not only armed force but also any other form of interference or attempted threat against the personality of the state or against its political or economic or cultural elements." It would hardly have been possible to make a more sweeping commitment of an anti-imperialist character.

At no time since the signing of these three agreements has the American government intervened by force of arms at any place in the New World. In 1938 it bore tolerantly the expropriation of American oil interests in Mexico and in Bolivia. In 1940 it made no protest against the Cuban constitution, which dealt harshly in some respects with American interests. Only once has the pledge given in the Montevideo, Buenos Aires, and Bogota protocols, even by a broad construction, been violated: this was in 1961. At that time there had been established in Cuba a government under Fidel Castro which formed a close connection with Communist Russia and Communist China, and which was itself Communist or proto-Communist in character. In April 1961, the American government gave encouragement and some measure of actual military and economic support to an attempted invasion of the island by counterrevolutionaries. Its action failed; it met with considerable criticism at home; and the Kennedy administration, notwithstanding provocations of an extreme character, reiterated previous pledges that it would take no direct hostile action against the Castro regime. This episode might raise the question (which only the future will resolve) as to whether the United States is bound to stand by while American governments are subverted with the encouragement and open aid of its avowed antagonists. It can hardly serve to shake the thesis that in its relations with its Latin American neighbors the United

States has demonstrated a restraint such as has only rarely been practiced by a nation possessed of great physical power. Moreover, it is one thing to abstain from interference with the freedom of action of the New World republics; it is another thing to permit the subversion of the free and independent states of the New World by international Communism.

A second aspect of United States relations with its "southern neighbors" should be mentioned. During the Second World War, by arrangement with other governments, notably Guatemala, Ecuador, Panama, and Brazil, its armed forces were stationed on the soil of these states. Today they are to be found in none of them. Even in the case of Panama, where an important security interest is plainly at stake, the American government, after long negotiations, withdrew its forces from Panamanian territory.

What was the record of the United States towards its conquered enemies at the end of the Second World War? What of Germany and Japan? In both cases the American government smiled upon the establishment of democratic regimes. In no way, once these regimes had been established, did it attempt to control them. True, American troops remain on German and Japanese soil. But they are there by agreement with the states concerned. They are there not as agents of control, but as symbols of the readiness of the American government to sustain the forces of popular rule. To speak of this as imperialism would be an absurdity.

One reservation must be made. In the islands of the Pacific conquered from Japan (of which Okinawa is the most important), the concern of our own military and naval men for security has resulted in the continuation of American administration. The treaty of peace with Japan, however, provided for the establishment of a United Nations trusteeship. As of the present writing, this provision has not been implemented. Yet the very willingness of the United States, in theory at least, to accept something less than unlimited sovereignty is a partial answer to its critics, and if the country follows precedents established, let us say, in the case of Guam, it will give a substantial voice to the inhabitants of these territories in the determination of their own affairs.

Up to this point we have been considering imperialism only in its political aspects. Now we must examine it on the economic side. Here, the questions that call for an answer are these: Where American political control or supervision has been extended, have the results been beneficial to the inhabitants of the area concerned, looking at the matter from the economic point of view? Second, have American business interests exercised—and do they exercise—a substantial and noxious control over the governments of other states in which they do business? And third, are the policies of the United States today, in America, in Europe, or in Asia, justly to be criticized as examples of "economic imperialism"?

To the first of these questions the answer seems clear. Such countries as Puerto Rico and the Philippines could almost certainly not have found the capital for their own development if they had operated as independent governments from 1898 thenceforward. They would have remained, as they then were, relatively backward communities. American rule gave to American capitalists the assurance of peace and order, and indeed of protection against arbitrary exaction, and thus contributed powerfully to encourage investment on a substantial scale. The case becomes still stronger when we are talking of regions in which chronic misgovernment existed before American control. You cannot expect foreign money to enter a country where disorder is virtually endemic. Whatever else American rule in the Dominican Republic may have done, to cite one example, it most certainly paved the way for a period of domestic tranquillity and opened the door to American entrepreneurs. The progress of the island since the American occupation has been remarkable, and it has had a far larger national income than before. Though the gain was less spectacular in Nicaragua or in Haiti, there, also, the net result of the American occupation was undoubtedly an economic advance.

It will be said that the profits from a situation of this kind go to a very few. That they are equitably distributed (assuming that we could agree upon what the word "equitably" implies), I should not for a moment attempt to assert. But that *some* benefit trickles down to a portion of the masses is certain. In the countries we have mentioned, American entrepreneurs usually pay higher wages than native employers and take better care of those who work for them. By their expanding activities, the number of workers is increased. The taxes which are levied upon them may go, if the government is honestly administered, or even if it is not, serve the public interest and to make social progress possible without imposing an undue burden upon the less fortunate class in the community. There is, undeniably, a net economic gain which extends beyond the narrow circle of the entrepreneurs themselves.

Nor can we entirely neglect other contributions that are sometimes made by an occupying power which indirectly promote the welfare of those temporarily under its rule. The United States, in its brief period of control in Cuba, did much to set going a system of public instruction and to check the ravages of yellow fever. It did something for education in the Dominican Republic. It did much for the building of roads in both the Dominican Republic and Haiti. It reorganized the railroad system in Nicaragua. And it provided in every case a domestic tranquillity which could hardly fail to be of value to the mass of the population, for it certainly means something to relieve the average man of the plunder of revolutionary armies and the depredations of civil war. In addition to all this, the United States has often expended its own funds on a very substantial scale to assist the economies of such communities as the Virgin Islands, Puerto Rico, and the Philippines.

The second question which we posed concerned the influence of American business corporations in countries where they do business but where there is no political control by the United States itself. There are undeniably shoddy episodes in the American past in this regard. The most reprehensible have to do with the fomenting of revolution or with the giving of support to revolutionary factions, of course with the hope of return if these factions come into power. The revolution of 1910 in Nicaragua, to cite a case, was beyond much question instigated by American interests on the east coast of the republic, and there was a connection, though a tenuous one, between these interests and the State Department. In the course of the next year, the revolution which broke out in Honduras was financed from New Orleans, and those who promoted it naturally had interested objects in view. In the Mexican turmoil of the period 1910 to 1917, the oil companies at times maintained private armies which bid defiance to the authority of the state, and some of them heavily backed the so-called Constitutionalists, participating actively in what was virtually a civil war. Less reprehensible, no doubt, but still not to be defended, are the cases, not innumerous in the history of the Central American republics in the same and in an earlier period, when fantastic privileges were secured by foreign corporations from complacent or corrupt legislatures, and when corporate influence was often powerful enough to permit the circumvention or defiance of the law.

To judge from the surface evidence, this kind of thing is far less likely to occur today. In the first place, the standard of American business morals, while not so high as to please the exacting, has undeniably improved. In the second, since the Latin American states (in which most of these episodes have occurred) are now protected against intervention by the United States by the protocols of Montevideo and Buenos Aires, they can make a more effective resistance to the exactions of foreign capitalists. To state the matter in another way, the capital-receiving state can and does prescribe the terms under which the foreign entrepreneur operates. The American government has left and does leave to other countries wide latitude in the fixing of these terms. It has, invariably, contented itself with formal protests and demands for compensation, even in cases of expropriation. It is bound not to intervene by physical force. It rests, then, with the capital-receiving state to form its policies so that, on the one hand, by inordinate exactions it does not kill the goose that lays the golden eggs and, on the other hand, it appropriates for its own people a reasonable part of the profits that come from foreign enterprise.

It is entirely wrong to regard the export of American capital to other lands as in itself immoral or exploitative. On the contrary, it is of the very essence of economic progress that states with a surplus of fluid capital use it to develop the economies of those which do not, that those who have the best managerial skills and technological know-how use these skills and this knowledge to develop the resources of lands less fortunate in their capacity to act for themselves.

Certainly, there must be some basis of understanding between the foreign entrepreneur and the state in which he operates. The entrepreneur must not be grasping; he must operate his business with some regard for the climate of opinion and for the social interests inevitably connected with his activities; the state must, on its part, not be oppressive in its policies and must recognize that those who invest their funds within its borders must not be prevented from making a fair profit on their investment. But with these things understood, the practice of capital export is beneficent, not maleficent—more, we repeat, it is indispensable to world progress. This fact should be self-evident. Unhappily it is not. The cliché "economic imperialism" is used to make odious what is normal and desirable. We need very emphatically to put this cliché in its place and to analyze very carefully the thought of those who put it forward.

This brings us to the third question asked at the beginning of our discussion: are American public policies today on the economic side rightly subject to criticism as imperialistic?

In the course of the last few years, the export of private capital has been supplemented—or supplanted—by the export of *public* capital. Should such capital export fall under moral condemnation? Was the Marshall Plan reprehensible, as our enemies asserted? I do not see how this question can be answered in the affirmative. True, the American grants of aid to European states implied some concession to American opinion on the part of the receiving states. But how could aid be given on any other terms? Is it not reasonable to ask assurances that it be used for the ends for which it is granted, and in a way that will assist the purposes we have in view? When and by what government would aid be given on any other basis? Is there any evidence that majority opinion in the countries aided, fully and freely expressed, regarded the conditions as unduly onerous? Was the national independence of the states concerned seriously curtailed? Was there any great national revolt against the acceptance of our support? Or is it not more likely that Europeans would say of the Marshall Plan, as Churchill did of Lend-Lease, that it was one of the most unsordid acts in history? It is a distortion of terms to apply the word "imperialism" to such an expedient of European recovery as the Marshall Plan.

What applies to the Marshall Plan applies no less to the military and economic grants made by the American government in various parts of the world. It is elementary that these grants should be something more than mere handouts; their beneficiaries can hardly object to provisions which guard against misuse and ensure the attainment of the purpose the United States has in view. It would indeed be a verbal topsy-turvydom in which arrangements freely entered into for the defense or economic stimulation of other states were represented as "imperialism." The fact that some confused minds accept such a definition proves nothing, except the melancholy ability of some of us to accept the illogical.

There is, finally, the vague term "moral imperialism." It is difficult to invest this phrase with exact content. Perhaps the nearest we can come to it is to deal with the problem of recognition. Historically, the American government has sometimes abstained from recognition of regimes whose moral origins it did not approve. The Central American treaties of 1907, negotiated with the encouragement of the State Department, called for the withholding of recognition of revolutionary regimes until free elections had taken place. Woodrow Wilson declined to recognize the Mexican ruler, Victoriano Huerta, because his rise to power was stained by the murder of his enemies. The Roosevelt administration refused to deal in 1944 with an Argentine government it did not believe representative of the Argentine people. The Soviet regime was recognized by the United States only in 1933, nearly sixteen years after its establishment. Other examples might be cited, including the consistent refusal of Washington to acknowledge the Chinese government at Peiping. Such pressure, it may be conceded, has in most instances been rather futile. Indeed, the practice of withholding recognition on moral grounds has been very largely abandoned. Only in the case of Communist China, which is still technically at war with the United States and which has violated many of the terms entered into for a truce in Korea, has the American government steadily refused to enter into formal relations with a regime of which it disapproves. Whatever one may think of the practice, the record of experience does not suggest that this type of moral imperialism constitutes a serious danger to the integrity or the continuance or the effective international action of the state against which it is directed.

In this review of American policy, it is not pretended that the record is above reproach. In the Philippines sharp hostilities preceded the establishment of American rule. In Haiti, Santo Domingo, and Nicaragua there was substantial local resistance to American authority. Our relations with Cuba are not without blemish. But, nonetheless, by the comparative standard, the United States has no reason to apologize for its record.

One other aspect of the problem of imperialism may be mentioned. What has been the attitude of the United States towards the imperialism of others? Has it been the stalwart defender of rule imposed from above, or has it been the champion of wider freedom? On the whole, it has been the latter. It favored the independence of India and of Indonesia. It has not been unfriendly to the establishment of the new and independent states of Africa. Its influence was exerted to encourage British withdrawal from Egypt. On occasion, caught between the interests of its European allies and its sympathy with self-determination, it has not always spoken so clearly. Yet its own example pleads strongly in its behalf. Its own imperialist impulse came late and, as we have seen, was soon exhausted. It does not lie with the Soviet Union to direct reproaches against it.

Powerful nations, by the ineluctable necessities of international politics, almost inevitably make their power felt. The question is, how do they exert it? Do they exert it with utter ruthlessness, as did Hitlerian Germany? Do they assert the universal validity of the principles on which their own governments are founded, as the Russian government does today? Do they intrigue to subvert regimes which they do not find attractive? Or are they led towards tolerance, as the United States has clearly been in accepting the doctrine of nonintervention in Latin America, and as it has shown in its attitude towards other forms of government in various parts of the world, until some issue of national security was involved? Have they used their economic power harshly, or towards goods ends? The answer to these questions suggests that, in the moderation that ought to go with strength, the United States on the whole has played and is playing a creditable role.

III

Capitalism and American Foreign Policy

———————◆·◄◆►·◆———————

EUROPEANS regard America as the land of business par excellence. From this assumption it is easy to proceed to the point of view that American foreign policy is based upon the interests of the capitalist class. It is also easy, provided the critic starts from a somewhat leftist slant, to believe that these interests are usually sinister in their influence and their effects. It is the object of this chapter to analyze these hypotheses.

In the first place, we must be careful to define what we mean by "capitalist." The term may easily be given a wide or a narrow definition. It is in a somewhat narrow sense that I shall here consider it. For a large part of its history the United States was predominantly an agricultural nation, and the dominant political force was that of the farmer and, in much of the North and in the West, of the small farmer. In one sense, it is true, this small farmer was a capitalist. But in the sense that the term is usually used today, this was hardly the case. The "cultivators," as Jefferson called them, were independent entrepreneurs, not large-scale employers, the owners of real estate, not of personalty. Their role in the formation of foreign policy will not be considered here. Nor shall I devote attention to the impact upon foreign policy of the great slaveholders. I shall confine myself to discussing the role of the masters of fluid capital and the masters of the industrial machine, and shall inquire into what has been their actual influence upon the conduct of foreign affairs.

We must, however, begin with a word of warning. One of the weaknesses of the economic interpretation of history is that it often assumes the existence of a monolithic class which acts as a unit in its influence upon policy. In truth, the interests of one capitalistic group may run counter to the interests of another capitalistic group; in a single group there may be divergences of opinion as to where self-interest really lies, or personal rivalries may distort or hamper action. In attempting very broadly to trace the influence of the men of finance, trade, and industry upon American diplomacy, we must be well aware at the outset that our generalizations are true only with reservations and would, in a more extended analysis, need to be substantially qualified. Nonetheless, it is possible to perceive broad tendencies which are worth observing and discussing.

In the early period of American history, the principal interests that fall within the general scope of our examination were the commercial rather than the industrial interests. It was they, for example, which dominated the foreign policy of the Washington administration and directed the rapprochement with Great Britain that was represented by the Jay Treaty of 1794. Their influence on government was naturally curtailed with the advent of the Democratic Republicans to power. Yet in Jefferson's administration the Tripolitan War was undertaken for the protection of commerce, and although the trading interests suffered much from the policy of commercial restriction pursued by Jefferson and Madison, they secured very substantial recognition in the treaty of 1815 with Great Britain, which, for the first time, placed the intercourse of the two countries on a footing of genuine equality. In the formulation of policy in the Monroe administration, the commercial classes had no unimportant part, for the Secretary of State under the fifth President was that sturdy New Englander, John Quincy Adams. In the question of the recognition of the Spanish-American colonies, Adams, as his diplomatic papers show, was keenly aware of the possible advantages to American trade. And in his attitude towards the breakdown of the colonial system, in his denunciation of that system as "an abuse of government," Adams reflected the point of view of the traders, as he did in the assertion of the noncolonization principle in the message of December 2, 1823. In the same way, in the cabinet meetings of the fall of the same year, in which was discussed the possible reconquest of the Spanish colonies, the Secretary of State, it is clear, while depreciating the danger, was concerned lest any action in behalf of Spain result in the establishment of the old colonial monopolies. Naturally, Monroe's famous declaration was dictated by larger interests than those of trade, but solicitude for American commerce nonetheless played a part in its enunciation.

In the years that followed one sees the influence of the same economic interests in the making of commercial treaties and in the first signs of active diplomacy in both the Near and the Far East. The treaty of 1831 with Turkey, the very important compact with China in 1844—and more than either—the dramatic mission of Perry to Japan, which broke down the isolation of the island empire and paved the way for expanding intercourse, were all signs of the importance of the traders in the evolution of American diplomacy. In the same period closer relations with Hawaii illustrated the same tendencies.

In the period after the Civil War a very substantial internal development and the increasing industrialization of the nation made the role of the merchant classes somewhat less important. But by the 1880's, an increasing concern with regard to our relations with Latin America and the calling of the abortive Pan-American conference of 1881 were signs that our foreign commerce was once again an object of governmental solicitude. Still more, at the turn of the century, the development of the Open-Door Policy by Secretary Hay looked in the same direction. Indeed, it has been pointed out in this connection that a small pressure group of American exporters to North China organized a powerful propaganda which apparently had its effect upon the Secretary of State. In more recent times, the desire to stimulate foreign trade has been reflected in many ways. In the course of the latter half of the nineteenth century, and well into the twentieth, American tariff policy was obstinately protectionist. Signs of a change only began to appear in the last days of the McKinley administration and in such measures as the reciprocity pact with Canada in 1911 (which, however, failed of adoption on the other side of the border). By the time of Franklin Roosevelt, Congress had in some degree moved away from the old economic nationalism. The various reciprocal trade agreement acts, inadequate though they were, paved the way for some reduction of duties and for some expansion of American international trade. Moreover, in the American reaction to the rising imperialisms of Germany and Japan, one element, though by no means the only one, was dislike of the restrictive trade policies of the totalitarian states. Japan threatened to close what was often assumed to be the vast potential market of China to the United States. A Europe dominated by Hitlerian Germany would offer very little opportunity for the advancement of American commerce. Few Secretaries have insisted more earnestly and more eloquently upon the necessity for the freer exchange of commodities than did Secretary Hull. That this theme was by no means the only factor in the development of American hostility to the dictators is patent, but that it has some significance is not to be denied.

There is one special aspect of foreign economic policy that ought not to be omitted from consideration here: the role of the tariff. The matter cuts deep, and among other things it amply illustrates the folly of thinking in monolithic terms of the influence of the "capitalists." The rivalry between the protected manufacturers and the importers and exporters runs throughout American history.

The protective tariff made its appearance from the beginning of the government. The nullification controversy of Andrew Jackson's time turned on just this question, on the interests of some of the Northern manufacturers, on the one hand, and of the cotton factors (who sold a great part of their crop abroad), on the other. In the period just before the Civil War, however, the tendency of the times was towards lower duties. The war itself precipitated a change. Internal taxes were balanced with protective duties, and when the struggle was over, the internal taxes were removed and the duties retained. For a time there was no great movement towards raising them. But by the end of the eighties the tariff question had become one of the central issues between the Republican and Democratic parties. Since the Republicans were, down to 1933, the majority party of the nation, the trend was for the most part upward.

The Payne-Aldrich Bill of 1909, the Fordney-McCumber Bill of 1922, and the Hawley-Smoot Bill of 1930 were all measures of exaggerated protectionism, in which the American interest in international trade was neglected. Tariffs became a means of swapping favors among the members of Congress, and since many districts had some small interest in protection, it was not strange that duties mounted.

But there came a change with the New Deal and with the Reciprocal Trade Agreements Act of 1934. By this measure the President was authorized, on the basis of reciprocity, to negotiate treaties reducing tariffs by 50 percent and, what was equally important, it was provided that the concessions made to the treaty power would be extended to every other nation. In 1945 Congress authorized the President to negotiate further reductions up to another 50 percent. By this means the old log-rolling process by which tariffs had previously been enacted was brought to an end and the power of lowering duties confided to the President. The interests of the international traders were thus substantially advanced.

The pressure of local interests has never ceased, however. As early as 1943 there was introduced into some of the agreements negotiated an "escape clause" which permitted the raising of duties in cases where serious injury to domestic producers was caused or threatened, and in the revision of the law in 1948 Congress provided by legislation for such increases on the recommendation of the Tariff Commission. Since then, other means of hampering the movement for lower duties have been devised. What the long-term effect of these limitations will be remains to be determined, but their very existence is a factor limiting the movement for freer trade.

But the interests of international trade are by no means

the only international interests connected with the so-called capitalists. We have to consider also the role of investment, either in the form of the actual establishment of American economic activities in some other state or in the form of loans to foreign governments. What has been the attitude of the government towards these activities?

For a substantial part of our history the United States was not a capital-exporting nation. It was not until the 1880's that American business began to seek opportunities abroad on any important scale, with Mexico, Cuba, and Hawaii as the first countries to arrest attention. The movement of capital was much accelerated in the period of American imperialism, and still more by the great expansion that followed the First World War. On the other hand, there was a distinct check to the process in the period of the thirties. Since the end of the Second World War, foreign investment has again substantially increased, reaching a total figure of more than $20 billion by the end of the decade of the fifties. It should be emphasized, however, that this is a small amount compared with the total of American investment at home.

What has been the actual influence of the American investor in foreign parts upon the course of American diplomacy? How far has the government intervened to protect the investor's interest? Clearly, it is the business of every government to see that its businessmen are accorded opportunities and reasonable treatment in foreign lands. In a brief essay we cannot possibly examine the innumerable cases in which the United States has made diplomatic representations to other governments in behalf of its investors; we must confine our analysis to those cases in which it has gone beyond this sphere and in one way or another taken more positive action for the protection of capitalist interests.

There are many instances in which such action enters into the story. The Open-Door Policy, for example, began with an attempt to prevent discrimination in matters of trade. It was soon extended—though not very successfully —in an effort to prevent the growth of spheres of influence in China and to secure a field for American investment there. At the Washington Conference in 1922 there was written into the so-called Nine-Power Treaty an agreement which bound the signatory states not to seek "any arrangement which might purport to establish in favor of their interests any general superiority of rights with respect to commercial or economic development in any designated region of China, or any . . . monopoly . . . calculated to frustrate the practical application of the principle of equal opportunity."

In the Caribbean and in Mexico, the United States has sought to promote the interest of investors in ways different from those employed in the Far East. In these regions a serious threat to capital came from the repeated revolutionary uprisings to which some of these countries were subject. In an effort to encourage internal stability in Central America, the United States sponsored in 1907 a remarkable agreement by which the signatory states agreed not to recognize any government of revolutionary origin, and a new agreement along similar lines was negotiated in 1923. With the same purpose of preserving domestic peace, the United States has sometimes denied arms to revolutionary factions, as in Mexico in 1912 and again in 1923–4, or permitted the shipping of arms to a faction which it deemed friendly to American interests, as in Nicaragua in 1927. On occasion, as in the case of the Obregon regime in Mexico in 1923, it has withheld recognition of an established government until reassured as to the treatment to be accorded to American capital. It has landed marines for the protection of American property, in Cuba in 1912 and 1917 and in Costa Rica in 1919, to cite three examples.

It is doubtful, however, whether the full-fledged interventions in Haiti, in the Dominican Republic, and in Nicaragua were carried out because of the pressure of American investors. It is difficult to dogmatize on such a matter, but the amount of American capital in these three states was trivial at the time that interference took place, and the fear of foreign interference and preoccupation with strategic interests apparently were much greater factors in stimulating action than were any small American capital holdings on the spot. Similarly, it would be difficult to show that economic considerations account for the action of the United States in the Spanish-American War. True, American sugar interests were for the most part in favor of intervention. But the widespread national sentiment against Spain can hardly be traced to this single source, or explained on any such restricted ground.

Nor must it be imagined that the United States has by any means always manifested a tender solicitude for the capital-exporting section of the community. The most striking case of an opposite policy has to do with Mexico. Despite the pressure of private interests, both the Taft and the Wilson administrations refused to intervene in that troubled republic in the second decade of the century. The business-minded Coolidge administration blustered a little when Mexican policy seemed to be unduly disregardful of American property rights, but it soon turned towards a more conciliatory policy. Under Franklin D. Roosevelt's regime, the Mexican expropriation of the oil companies and wide-spread seizures of agricultural lands in the hands of Americans produced only relatively mild protests, and they were finally adjusted on a basis which most certainly could not be said to be extravagantly generous to the private owners involved. Indeed, the climate of opinion in the United States during the last thirty years cannot be said to have favored extreme policies with regard to the rights of American investors abroad. Quite the contrary, indeed, is the case, as is well illustrated by the American acceptance of the non-intervention principle at Montevideo and Buenos Aires. A still more striking illustration is the reluctance of the American government to intervene in Cuba after the wholesale confiscations of American property by Fidel Castro in 1959 and 1960.

Up to this point, we have been speaking of those capitalists who actually invested their funds in business activities in other states. But there is, too, a second type of businessman, the banker. What role have the bankers played in American foreign policy? It would be difficult to show that they had, in any sense, dominated the course of events. For a long time—in fact down to the beginning of the twentieth century—external loans played no great part in the development of the American economy. The early ones were made in obedience to the desires of government rather than from any strong drive on the part of the bankers themselves. In the Caribbean area the policies of the Theodore Roosevelt and the Taft administrations were directed towards removing the danger of foreign intervention for the collection of debts, with its possible threat of the long-time occupation of American territory. To ward off these dangers, the United States entered into agreements for the reorganization of the finances of one or another of the little states in these regions, assuming the control of the customs and exercising some supervision over their finances. The impetus of action came, surely in very substantial degree, from the State Department and *not* from Wall Street. Let us look at the policy pursued in Nicaragua. In 1911 Secretary Knox negotiated a treaty with this state which provided for the kinds of control just mentioned. In advance of the ratification of this arrangement—a ratification which was long delayed—he persuaded a New York banking house to make a loan to the then existing Nicaraguan government. The amount that was involved was by no means large, nor was the rate of interest extravagant. The bankers acted in the furtherance of a policy that was strategic rather than financial. Unhappily, revolution broke out before long in Nicaragua; and the American government intervened, as it was almost bound to do, to protect the bankers' investment which it had urged upon them. It set up a government that would do what it wanted to see done; and its supervision of Nicaraguan politics lasted, with a brief interruption, until 1929. That it saw to it that a further loan was made, and that it was properly serviced, is true; but here again the motive was by no means that of providing profits for a special economic group, but rather of restoring the Nicaraguan economy. "The motives for the original entry of the United States into Nicaragua," says J. W. Angell in *The Financial Foreign Policy of the United States,* "have been primarily strategic and political and to some extent genuinely philanthropic." This seems to me a fair statement of the matter.

Much the same considerations had a part in the cases of Haiti and the Dominican Republic. Here again it was at the solicitation of the State Department that the National City Bank of New York became in 1910 one of the participators in the reorganization of the Haitian Banque Nationale; and, once this reorganization had been effected, a continuation of internal disorders in the Negro republic led to intervention. But again, to quote Professor Angell, "the judgment which is passed on the American policy towards Haiti and its effects must rest on factors not lying primarily in the field of finance." Behind the activities of Secretary Knox, we repeat, lay a concern lest foreign capital in the Caribbean lead to the interference of European powers in an area of great importance to the defense of the United States. The policy pursued towards the Dominican Republic would illustrate the same general tendencies.

In the Orient, too, the impetus to foreign lending came in no inconsiderable degree from government. In 1909 the Taft administration attempted to persuade a number of American banking interests to participate in a consortium, at that time composed only of British, French, and German interests, with the motive of strengthening the American position in the Far East. In the formal sense it was successful. But the bankers showed no great enthusiasm for the suggested enterprise, and, when the Wilson administration entered office and declined to request American financial participation in a new loan, the banking interests made no great difficulty about accepting the decision. It was never possible after the end of the First World War to arouse any enthusiasm in Wall Street for participation in Chinese financial affairs.

In the decade of the twenties, American foreign policy encouraged the flotation of the Dawes and Young Plan loans for the reconstruction of Germany and for the facilitation of reparations payments. But in general, for this period as for the earlier one, it would be difficult to show that the bankers profoundly influenced governmental policy. High protective tariffs were directly opposed to their interests; yet the tariff was raised just after the war and still further raised in 1930. In some instances the American government discouraged foreign lending in order to bring pressure to bear on European governments that had made no real effort to settle their public indebtedness to the United States. Still more, the State Department would assume no positive responsibility with regard to foreign loans, though claiming the right to express an opinion with regard to their political expediency. The very substantial pecuniary advances that were made in this period, some of them reckless, as the event proved, were in no sense encouraged by Washington, nor were any important steps taken to protect the lenders when default came.

When we come to the Roosevelt administration, we may say with assurance that it was extremely lukewarm in its support of the bondholders; in this matter it undoubtedly reflected the set of American opinion. It did little more than to give a kind of tepid approval to the establishment of a private organization known as the Council of Foreign Bondholders, set up to see what it could rescue from the defaults of the previous years. With regard to this matter, as with regard to capital export in the business sense, it tied its own hands by its acceptance of the principle of nonintervention.

As for the situation today, there is certainly no great enthusiasm among the members of the financial class for large-scale loans abroad. These people had their fingers burned in the twenties and early thirties and are of no mind to burn them again. The establishment of public agencies like the International Bank and the Export-Import Bank seems to indicate that international lending is more and more likely in the future to be directed by government itself, rather than made the concern of private interests. This is not to say that there will be no private loans whatever; it is merely to say that it is difficult to believe that the great money-lenders will care to assume sweeping responsibilities or that government will encourage them to do so.

Were we to sum up the ground already traversed, we should, I think, say that commercial interests have often exercised a substantial influence upon American policy; that American business established on foreign soil has exercised an influence far less; and that the bankers have exercised the least influence of all. But there is a wider question that ought to be discussed in this essay, and that is the question as to whether the "capitalists" have, on the whole, tended to support peaceful or bellicose policies. We have already seen that the commercial classes were in favor of accommodation with Britain in the days of the Washington administration. In the main, they continued to maintain this view for a substantial time thereafter, and, in 1812, New England, which in theory had the greatest stake in the protection of American rights at sea, was in practice that part of the country which was most lukewarm (if lukewarm is a strong enough term) with regard to the whole conflict. In the period down to the Civil War, it was probably the Whigs who represented the interests of the capitalists (though this generalization is subject to qualification), and the years of Whig domination of the government were years of a conciliatory foreign policy. The first period (1841–43) saw the negotiation of the Webster-Ashburton Treaty with Great Britain. The second saw the negotiation of the Clayton-Bulwer Treaty. The instinct for compromise in both of these compacts was strong—too strong, some distinguished students of American foreign policy believe.

In the period after the Civil War, the business interests were assuming a greater and greater role in American affairs; yet there has rarely been a more peaceful period. From 1870 to 1890 the tranquillity of the country was rarely troubled and never really seriously disturbed. Nor was it the business interests, speaking in the broad sense, that provoked the war with Spain. J. W. Pratt has analyzed their attitude with much skill in his *Expansionists of 1898*. He has shown that men like President McKinley and his mentor Mark Hanna, the very prototypes of business-minded politicians, were eager for peace, and he has also demonstrated that down to March of 1898, while the sentiment of the country became more and more bellicose, the business classes, as their views were reflected in the commercial journals, were less war-minded than many others. True, the mood changed as the clash of arms approached, but it would certainly not be reasonable to say that the struggle with Spain was provoked principally by the men of money.

It has sometimes been charged that business interests were behind the entry of the United States into the First World War. The charge, for a time, took hold, and it was widely believed. It seems worth while, therefore, to analyze this matter in some detail. The argument runs as follows: America early became involved in an important commerce with the Allies, in a detestable munitions traffic and in an even wider commercial support of the Allied cause. In due time, too, loans began to be floated in this country on an increasing scale, and the stake of the United States (i.e., of the bankers and traders) in an Allied victory became more and more immense. It was to protect this trade and these loans that America finally went to war in 1917. It was Wall Street that dictated the course of action to Woodrow Wilson.

Perhaps it is not possible completely to put down this

belief because it is always difficult to prove a negative, and still more difficult to trace in all its infinite and subtle manifestations the evolution of American public opinion between 1914 and 1917. It seems reasonably clear, however, at least to this student of the period, that the assumption that the war of 1917 was a war of the financiers does violence to a good many of the essential facts. The actual *casus belli* in 1917, I imagine it would be generally conceded, was the German resumption of submarine warfare. This warfare, from the first, aroused widespread indignation in America. As we have seen, Wilson sought to limit its effects by diplomatic pressure on the German government, and in the spring of 1916, under threat of a severance of diplomatic relations, he actually brought Berlin to an abandonment of the U-boat campaign. But his victory was short-lived. In February of 1917, the German sea action was resumed, causing first a break in relations and then war. Now the question raised by this review of the essential facts in the controversy with Germany is simply this. How is it possible to prove that the United States would have entered the war if the government of the Reich had held its hand? As a matter of fact, in the electoral campaign of 1916, Woodrow Wilson was re-elected to the presidency of the United States on the very ground that he had kept us *out* of war. Our relations with Great Britain in the fall of 1916, as any student of this period could easily demonstrate, were less cordial than at any time since the outbreak of the struggle. The Irish rebellion and the arrogance of British action at sea had alienated many Americans and even provoked Congressional legislative action of a retaliatory character in the session of 1916. At the close of the year the Federal Reserve Board actually issued a warning against further extension of credit to the Allies. How do such facts as these fit in with the thesis that the financiers had the game in their hands? And how, I repeat, can it be asserted with any confidence that war would have come if the Germans had continued to mind their manners?

There are, of course, other difficulties with the proposition that the bankers were responsible for our entrance into the war. Let us look a little further at this matter of the submarine. Was Wilson's position on the submarine in any way dictated by financial interest, by the growth of Allied trade and the floating of Allied loans? Chronology makes necessary a negative answer to this question. Wilson took his stand against submarine warfare in the note of February 10, 1915, and reaffirmed it in the most solemn terms in his note of May 13 of the same year. But, at this time, no war loan had been issued, and the munitions trade itself was in its infancy. Nor is it at all consistent with any accurate interpretation of Wilson's character—or of the temper of the time—to imagine that the joining of the submarine issue was a mere cover for the protection of financial interests. The President was very far from business-minded, very, very far from being the darling of Wall Street. And, though it may seem strange to a generation habituated to every horror in connection with the prosecution of war that the submarine campaign shocked the American conscience in 1915, those who lived through those days can bear ready testimony to this fact. It would be nothing less than fantastic to charge the President with exploiting this specific issue to serve the purposes of the capitalists.

True, we must not push a thesis too far. It would not be right to say that financial interests had no influence on American policy in the period we are for the moment examining. The United States was emerging from a minor depression in 1914. The policy of withholding all credits from both sides, a policy advocated by William Jennings Bryan and actually put in effect in the early days of the war, was soon abandoned, and abandoned a bit surreptitiously and perhaps not in completely good conscience. The revival of American trade which came in 1915 and 1916 was exceedingly convenient for the administration. But it is an immense leap from a candid recognition of these facts to the thesis that the Wilson administration led the country into war at the behest of the financial interests.

With the end of the First World War we enter a period in which the influence of the "capitalists" was particularly felt in the administration of the government. This is the period of the Washington Conference for the reduction of naval armaments; it is a period of limited responsibility for the keeping of the peace in Europe, a period often described as "isolationist" and certainly not in any sense adventurous; it is the period of the Kellogg Pact for the outlawry of war. It is difficult to see in what respects these years give any evidence of bellicosity. On the contrary, concern with domestic profits and with economy in government was a more powerful motive with the business classes than any instinct towards wider dominion abroad.

It is possible to argue, with regard to the events of the thirties, as we have seen, that exclusion, or threatened exclusion, from great markets had something to do with the rise of war sentiment against Hitler and against Japan; but to think of this factor as the controlling one seems to be pushing matters entirely too far. The sentiment that sustained President Roosevelt in his policy of unneutrality and assistance to the Allies, that made him the champion of Chinese independence against the forces of Japanese militarism, that led, we must admit, towards the ultimate clash of arms, was drawn from all classes of the community and from widely different sections of the nation. It rested, as even the most superficial study would easily show, on a variety of factors: on the possible threat to American security posed by German and Japanese aggression, a threat underlined by the German-Japanese treaty of alliance of September 27, 1940, on detestation of the cynicism of the totalitarian states, on reprobation of their treatment of minorities, and on democratic principle. The business classes shared in many of these emotions; that they were thinking chiefly of their own interests would be very difficult to demonstrate.

For us today the foregoing analysis is related to questions of general principle. In our survey of the attitude of the business classes towards war and of their influence on foreign policy, we have been casting doubts on widely held hypotheses that are connected with what may be called the Marxist interpretation of foreign policy. Marxists have believed that capitalist societies are intrinsically bellicose and that the capitalist world is doomed either to an internal struggle or to perpetual wars of aggression out of which the world revolution will emerge. Our survey of American foreign policy has not—up to this point, at any rate—sustained this view, but we might examine the matter a little further.

The Marxists, it appears to me, have argued from false premises to debatable conclusions. There is no denying that the capitalist world has seen plenty of fighting; so, too, did the noncapitalist world of the Middle Ages; so, too, have many other human societies. But to assume that the explanation lies in the economic organization of society, rather than in something deeper and more intangible in the nature of man, is highly doubtful—indeed, doubtful on any of the hypotheses that the Marxians have put forward. Let us, for a moment, discuss these hypotheses.

One is connected with the name of Rosa Luxemburg. The Luxemburg doctrine suggests that the essence of the matter lies in the principle of underconsumption and that capitalist societies fall victim to the operation of a general law. In such societies wealth tends to accumulate in the hands of a few; the market for goods within the society tends to contract; and it becomes necessary for the capitalists to engage in projects of conquest and war in order to maintain and increase their profits.

This theory cannot possibly be reconciled with the facts of contemporary American life. It is simply not true that the rich are getting richer and the poor poorer. The division of the national income among the various economic groups in the community has shifted—though not in dramatic fashion—in favor of the less fortunate. The tax policies of the United States impose heavy and increasing burdens on the rich. The climate of opinion today is sharply critical of any tendency towards the accumulation of wealth in the hands of a few, and it is a commonplace to students of American history that the age of the greatest fortunes is behind, not before, us. Moreover, the opportunities for profit have by no means been exhausted. On the contrary, the extraordinary vitality of the American economy suggests that there are many excellent openings at home. The prospects of development within the boundaries of the country, through a multiplication of activities and an immense technological advance, are surely as great as the chances of expansion beyond our borders. This means that there can hardly be the urge to war on the part of the capitalist which Rosa Luxemburg envisioned.

But far more important than the theory of Rosa Luxemburg is the theory of Lenin. In his classic essay on imperialism, Lenin lays great emphasis on the growth of monopolies and on the merging of industrial capital with bank capital to create what he calls "finance capital." These great combinations naturally tend to look for an extension of their operations beyond their borders. Dominating the state as they do, while they may for a time share the world with each other, they will in the long run come to the point where they must force a great struggle of arms. To Lenin, as the above comments suggest, the political state is simply the instrument of the capitalist.

No more than Luxemburg's does Lenin's theory fit the facts of American life. Though it has without question played a part in American development, monopoly is not the characteristic form of American economic life today. There is not the combination of banking and industrial capital which the Russian theorist assumed to be fundamental. Lenin argued on this point from his observation of the German economic organization, and he was strongly influenced by the German writer, Hilferding. But in the United States there has never been a period when the great banking interests dominated the industrial life of the nation, though we were perhaps moving in that direction towards the end of the century, when such great houses as J. P. Morgan wielded an immense authority and control. Today commercial and investment banking have been separated from one another, and the great corporations are by no means the tools of the moneylenders. More important still, as we have seen, it simply is not true that the government is the tool of the bankers. The analysis which we have already made of this point is amply sufficient to refute the Leninist point of view.

There is another point to be made. Lenin's assumption that capitalist societies must inevitably war with one another cannot be completely refuted, for to deny his assumption implies a knowledge of the future such as cannot be claimed by the historian; it belongs only to the religious and secular prophets. But the tendency of our times is otherwise. The great non-Communist states themselves have coalesced against the danger which is implicit in the developing power of the Soviet Union. The possibility of their engaging in war against one another has never been less than it is today.

A third version of the Marxist gospel is that of Stalin, and it is perhaps best set forth in his famous declaration of February 1946. Here the emphasis is on the danger of collapse in the capitalist countries; this collapse leads to fascism, and fascism leads to war, war against those virtuous lands in which another form of economic organization prevails. It is a commonplace that the Soviet leaders eagerly expected that collapse at the end of the war; and by this time they must be somewhat discontented that it has not come to pass. Of the validity of the general theory we shall have something more to say in another chapter. But it might well be observed here that in practice Russian policy, by stimulating great expenditures in the capitalist countries, and above all in the United States, made deflation less likely rather than more so. Here again, a mere historian will not engage in dogmatism. But insofar as Stalin, like Lenin, definitely assumed that the American economic order is controlled by a few men who will seek to turn it to their own ends, we can take a stronger stand. The seat of political power does not rest in Wall Street. Labor exercises no small share of it; the farmer exercises no small share of it; business interests, small and large, exercise a part of it. No informed student of American life would suggest that this power was concentrated in, or that government pipes to the tune of, a sinister economic group. And here again the analysis already made in this chapter makes clear what has just been asserted.

Marxist theory is connected with the hypothesis that goes by the name of economic determinism and which assumes that economic forces are the decisive elements in the fashioning of state policy, foreign policy included. The catch here, of course, lies in the word "decisive." No informed historian would deny the significance of economic factors in the sphere of diplomacy. There have been ample evidences of this influence in what has already been said; there will be other evidences in some of the matters to be treated in later essays. But the question is not as to whether these influences exist; it is whether they are decisive. And how we answer this question is a matter of our mental constitutions, especially of our confidence in our own powers of evaluation. Surely, there are not many of us who would say the economic factor was "exclusive." Man is essentially a complex animal, moved by self-interest but subject also to strong emotional urges that may or may not run parallel with his economic interests, given to perverse intellectual judgments which, like his feelings, may not be the expression of his material desires or purposes, swayed by deep-seated faiths and loyalties, religious and secular, that hardly correspond with his desire to accumulate and to profit. Who can weigh with precision the factors that enter into his conduct of his affairs? What arrogance is involved in the attempt to try!

Of these factors one element is the moral one. In the next chapter we shall turn to a discussion of the role of moral conceptions in the formation of the foreign policy of the United States.

IV

The Moralistic Interpretation of American Foreign Policy

———————

THE realistic student of foreign affairs will perforce admit the very large role that is played by sheer physical power in the intercourse of nations. But those who assume that physical power operates apart from all other considerations, and especially apart from what may well be described as moral considerations, display a shallow kind of cynicism that is far removed from the facts. The most absolute and the most unscrupulous dictators are themselves the refutation of this point of view. In international affairs, as in life in general, hypocrisy is the tribute that vice pays to virtue. Adolf Hitler had no public morals whatsoever, so far as his diplomacy was concerned. Yet he constantly branded other people as warmongers in an effort to make war palatable to his own people; again and again he fabricated stories of atrocities suffered by Germans outside the Reich in order to give some kind of moral validity to his projects of aggrandizement; and he created an ideology around which loyalties could center in an opposition to Communism. In the same way the present leaders of the Soviet Union, while quite oblivious of any precepts of international morality, constantly talk in terms of such precepts, constantly invoke the Hitlerian device of describing other people as bellicose and sinister in their ambitions, pretend to be interested in disarmament while maintaining the largest armed forces in the world in proportion to their population, and make appeal to an ideology which becomes a kind of faith, with all the moral implications that faith implies and with the declared end the betterment of the fortunes of the human race. No government in the modern world could treat its people as if moral ideas did not exist, and none would try.

The degree, however, to which moral ideas influence diplomacy will vary, and the expression of these ideas will vary with the political constitution and mores of the individual state. In Hitlerian Germany or Soviet Russia, ethical concepts may be a mere device for the advancement of the national interests, a mere support to a largely cynical diplomacy. But we must not imagine that it is only in the dictatorships that this is true. It has been true of states which were not autocratic in form. In Europe in the nineteenth century, foreign policy was conducted very largely in secret and by professional diplomats, who acted independently, to a very large degree though not absolutely, without regard to public opinion. In such conditions it is not strange that there were many "deals," which were not supposed to see the light of day, and that agreements were often entered into which concerned third parties and perhaps sacrificed their interests, agreements which might have met with considerable condemnation if they had been made public. In general, putting the matter in another way, a very free hand was left to the professionals by the people themselves, and the professionals naturally made such use as they chose of this freedom, promoting the national interest as they understood it, no doubt, but referring to public opinion only when they felt compelled to do so, or when they found in it a useful support for their own objectives. Nor have we seen the last of professional diplomacy in our own age. There is still in many countries a long tradition of relative freedom of action for government in the conduct of foreign affairs, and while this tradition is no doubt declining in force, it is still a factor in the actual conduct of foreign relations.

In the United States, on the other hand, to a degree remarkable at least by comparison, a different way of thinking and acting with regard to these matters has developed. American democracy is not by any means precisely like the democracy of European states. There has not been a governing class in America since the Federalists aspired to that title at the end of the eighteenth century. The professional diplomat hardly existed in much of the nineteenth century, and he has never occupied the secure position that he once occupied, and to some degree still occupies, in the Old World. To an extent that is true in no other country, the motivating force in government has come up from the people, rather than down from a political or diplomatic elite. The average man in America, be he well informed or ill informed, is likely to think that he has a right to express an opinion in politics and to have that opinion considered. When complex issues are submitted to examination in such a mechanism as the *Fortune* poll, the amazing thing is often the small number of persons who will say that they do not know the answer. The spirit of American politics suggests that the citizen *does* know the answers, and, in any case, the citizen is likely to think that he knows. In addition to all this, there has been from the beginning of American politics (and here we anticipate what we are to examine in more detail later) a dislike of secrecy with regard to foreign affairs and a habit of public debate on foreign issues. The great questions of foreign policy have often been submitted to public debate, often discussed with great frankness from more than one point of view, and often decided by the test of public opinion. No one can understand American diplomacy who does not grasp the importance of the democratic motif in its historic evolution.

Now the mass of men are, of course, not equipped to understand in their infinite ramifications and details the problems that confront a nation in the field of foreign affairs. If they exercise an influence on policy (and it has just been stated they *do* exercise such an influence in America), they are almost bound, in the nature of the case, to attach themselves to relatively simple concepts, to principles easy to understand and relevant to their general democratic experience, or to emotional attitudes that spring from the circumstances of the moment. Among these considerations, for example, may be the idea that democratic government is the best government on earth (irrespective of the particular situation of a given nation), or the idea that conquest is inherently immoral (without too sharp a scrutiny of the American past in this regard), or the idea that it is wrong to negotiate in secret (though it is hard to see how diplomacy could be carried on if there were not at least some secrecy), or the idea that the state is bound by the same moral code as is the individual (though this is a knotty question even for philosophers). And if views such as these are widely diffused throughout the community, and if they are also strongly held, they are bound, of course, to affect the tone of our diplomatic action and to influence very strongly the actual conduct of our public men. In other words, principles, strongly fused with emotions, will play a very great part in the foreign policy of such a country as the United States. Because this is so (and again the point must be elaborated later), high-sounding declarations and general appeals to international morality will often characterize the utterances of our statesmen and even their private diplomatic notes. When we say this, we by no means imply that Americans are unique in this regard. But it is, I think, fair to say that there is a highly moralistic flavor to our diplomacy as compared with the other nations. To foreigners this lofty moral tone no doubt sometimes seems like cant or a mere device of the diplomats themselves. But these people do Americans injustice; and the best test of this is to be found in the fact that, on occasion, the government of the United States has put ethical considerations ahead of national interest as it would be defined in the narrow sense of the term.

Before we examine, however, the moralistic overtones in American diplomacy, we must pause to remark that these overtones do not necessarily and inevitably mean that American foreign policy is therefore "better" than the diplomacy of other nations, even if we maintained, which we do not, that the difference was one in kind and not in degree. For one thing, the oversimplification of the issues which results from an appeal to moral principle may or may not be desirable in practice. The conviction, for example, that democratic government is the best of all governments may lead us to try to impose it on others, without success and with the result that international irritation ensues. A moral repugnance to imperialism and conquest may blind Americans to the practical difficulties in the way of giving complete independence to nations not yet very well prepared for it. A dislike of secrecy may lead to a degree of publicity in international affairs which makes compromise difficult and which arouses rather than allays the passions that often play a part in international affairs. The notion that the state must be bound by the same code as the individual may lead to quixotic action and naive judgment in the real world of international affairs. Principles are both useful and dangerous, both inspiring and exacerbating.

Indeed, one of the major difficulties with the moralistic view of foreign policy is that it makes for rigidity. The business of diplomacy is often the business of adjusting rival interests and rival points of view, of giving a little here and there and of getting a little in return. But if every question is to be invested with the aura of principle, how is adjustment to take place? There is no more difficult problem in the world of individuals than that of bringing together contestants who, each from his own point of view, are clad in the armor of unsullied righteousness. The same thing applies to nations.

Furthermore, moral judgments, since they rest on a foundation of deep feeling, rather than on precise analysis, may and sometimes do verge on sentimentality. A moral judgment may be very naive in the manner in which it assesses the elements of a complex problem. It has been difficult for some good people to accept the fact that the ushering in of an era of good will is not a prime objective of foreign policy for the Soviet Union; they cannot persuade themselves that some such ethical objective does not underlie the action of the Kremlin, as it would, no doubt, underlie their own action if they were where they could act effectively. Or, to take another example, it was easy for most Americans to believe, more deeply than on the basis of the facts they ought to have believed, in the efficacy of the Kellogg Pact, by which nations who signed pledged themselves not to resort to war as an instrument of policy. The promise to be virtuous is not virtue, as the generation which followed discovered before long. In the field of international organization, too, Americans are sometimes deceived by their feelings. World government, for example, is an appealing ideal so long as one feels about it rather than thinks about it. But it is by no means certain that the institutional approach to peace is the best approach, and it is certainly not the only one.

It is not, however, the object of this essay to make a moral judgment on the moralistic approach of the Americans to diplomacy; it is rather my purpose, by reviewing the national story, to make clear how strong this moralistic emphasis has been and how often it has played a part in foreign policy. Let us look first of all at the strong influence exerted by the democratic ideal upon American action. And here we may begin with the events of the second Washington administration and with the difficulties of the first President in shaping a course which was to the interest of the nation. There seems to me little doubt about what was wise policy for the United States in this initial period. An intellectual or realistic view of the matter would surely have led to an understanding with Great Britain, our principal source of imports, our best customer, our neighbor in North America, and the holder of our border posts at a time when we were little equipped to afford the luxury of British hostility. So, of course, Washington viewed the matter; on this basis he acted in the despatch of the Jay mission. Yet such men as Jefferson and Madison, representing a powerful section of opinion, advocated measures of commercial reprisal against Great Britain, which would probably have been fruitless, and opposed bitterly the treaty of 1794. The basis of their action lay, without question, in their sympathy for the French Revolution—in other words, in ideological and moral considerations.

The revolutions in Latin America had a substantial repercussion in the United States. There were certainly many distinctions between the course of the events in that part of the world and the course of events at home. But the judgment of such an American as Henry Clay took none of these factors into account. In his speeches in Congress in 1818, he put great stress on the similarity of the institutions of North and South America, and laid the basis for the structure that was later to become known as Pan-Americanism. The more cautious and intellectual Adams saw a very different picture; he was influenced by motives at once more realistic and more selfish; and the recognition of the colonies, for which Clay clamored, was postponed till 1822, when the United States had safely acquired the Floridas from Spain. But the ideological note is strong, indeed, in the policy of the Monroe administration itself when we come to the famous declaration of December 2, 1823. In a sense, the message is an ideological tract, praising the democratic principle and exalting democratic forms in contrast to the monarchies of Europe. And if Monroe had had his way, its ideological character would have been still more complete, for he proposed to add to the message a sympathetic reference to the Greeks and a commentary on the suppression of constitutional government in Spain. Of course it is not to be contended that none but idealistic and moral considerations entered into Monroe's pronouncement. In one sense, it was based upon the principle of national security, on the assumption that the restoration of monarchical rule in Latin America was "dangerous to our peace and safety." But this hypothesis would have been difficult to prove if submitted to the acid test of analysis, especially at the time that the President issued his famous challenge. The prime significance of the message was ideological, and

its prime origin lay in Americans' feeling of moral association with their "southern brethren." Europeans clearly
recognized this fact; Metternich was by no means alone
among European conservatives in bewailing what he fore-
saw as the separation of the New World from the Old.
Indeed, any careful study of the period will make it clear
that the young republic of the West was regarded by Continental Europeans as having deliberately and arrogantly
laid down a principle which flew in the face of European
doctrine and which was primarily based on very different
assumptions from the assumption of legitimacy. The immense enthusiasm which the message aroused in the United
States, the press comment of the time, dwelt for the most
part very little upon the sense of immediate peril and very
much upon the distinction between the institutions of Europe and the institutions of America.

The moral factor in diplomacy, the sympathy with the
democratic ideal, was again expressed in the European revolutions of 1848. The American government acted promptly,
almost precipitately, in recognizing the Second French Republic in 1848. The Hungarian revolt was followed with
intense enthusiasm by many Americans, and the Taylor
administration sent an American representative to Hungary,
with instructions to hold out assurances of recognition if
the circumstances warranted. When the Austrian government protested this action, Secretary of State Daniel Webster responded in a despatch whose flowing periods and
flamboyant tone make it one of the most remarkable in
American diplomatic intercourse. And though with Russian
aid the independence movement was put down, the patriot
Kossuth, when he came to this country, was received with
transports of acclaim and honored by a banquet at which
Webster himself was one of the speakers. True, it was not

possible for Americans to do anything effective; armed intervention was out of the question, for reasons of geography, if nothing else; but the tension created by this episode was great enough to lead to a temporary interruption of relations between the Austrian minister and the Secretary of State.

The clash of political ideals was again illustrated in the course of events in Mexico in the fifties and the sixties. In the struggle between the liberal and reactionary elements in that country, the United States was naturally impelled to take the side of the liberals. It supported the Juarez regime from an early period, and the Buchanan administration even went so far as to negotiate what was virtually a treaty of protectorate with that regime. French intrigues in behalf of monarchy, from the first regarded with suspicion, became the object of pointed reprobation on the part of Seward even in the course of the Civil War, and they aroused such widespread indignation during that struggle that in April 1864 the House of Representatives passed unanimously a resolution condemning the policy of Napoleon III. And, at the end of the war, there was still more emphatic expression of public sentiment, which might conceivably have led to war had it not been for the adroit diplomacy of Seward and the reaction in France itself against the adventure in Mexico.

The theme of democratic idealism runs through the whole history of Pan-Americanism, which began to find expression in positive form with James G. Blaine. The economic determinist will doubtless discover ulterior motives behind the calling of the Latin American conference of 1889; and such motives there undoubtedly were. But would it have been possible to weld together the nations of the New World in so close an association on the basis of a trade infinitely less significant than that with Europe? Is it not certain that the belief, whether justified or not, that there existed a similarity of institutions among the states of North and South America had something to do with the success of this important movement? And have not Pan-American conferences again and again asserted the validity of democratic principles and paid tribute to the democratic ideal?

Nor is this the only way that the United States has attempted to promote democracy on this side of the Atlantic. Sometimes it has gone further and attempted to use its influence more directly. The Central American treaties of 1907 and 1923, with their doctrine that governments arising from revolution ought not to be recognized, was, in a sense, an attempt to impose the American way of orderly election and popular choice upon some of our weaker neighbors. Largely ineffective in practice it has certainly been; today not many students of American diplomacy would advocate such policy. But this does not alter the fact that democratic principle affected action. Nor must we forget the still more striking case in which the same idea was applied: Woodrow Wilson's attitude towards Mexico. The refusal of the President to recognize the blood-stained regime of Victoriano Huerta was based squarely upon principle, and ironically enough this insistence on principle came very near to leading to intervention. No doubt Wilson's policy came in for very sharp criticism from some of those who described themselves as realists, but it was, nonetheless, resolutely adhered to, and it led, of course, to the fall of the Mexican dictator.

We have already discussed the interventions in the Caribbean. Here the motives, as we have seen, were largely strategic. But in every case, be it noted, the final act was an election conducted according to democratic principle, and the notion that somehow or other the unruly little peoples of this area could be instructed—and coerced—into accepting American conceptions of popular government was at all times present.

In the evolution of American public opinion with regard to the world war, a sense of democratic morality was certainly one of the factors that shaped the course of policy. Americans, from the beginning, contrasted the political institutions of France and Britain with the institutions of Germany. They were by no means always fair in this regard; to describe Germany as an autocracy in 1914 was stretching things pretty far. They overlooked, also, the fact that the Russian regime was far closer to political absolutism than the governments of the Central Empires. But although the generalization that the war was a struggle of autocracy against democracy had only a partial validity, this did not in any way diminish the force of the popular sentiment in this regard. The policy of partiality towards the Allies, and of discrimination against Germany, was in no small degree due to moral considerations. It explains why the Wilson administration dealt gently with British violations of international law and held rigidly to principle in dealing with the government in Berlin. It explains why the President himself, highly trained though he was, could echo the popular generalization in some of the very greatest of his speeches, and why he could proclaim the struggle to be in very truth a struggle involving political forms.

Wilson's war message, indeed, is largely based on this theory. Democratic governments, he seems to be saying, are peaceful governments; they act on principles of international morality different from those of autocratic governments. They do not (here Wilson was either misinformed or disingenuous) fill their neighbor states with spies; they do not embark upon ambitious enterprises of conquest. The peace of the world depends upon the breaking of the force of autocracy and upon the setting up of democratic regimes. "The world must be made safe for democracy." The President goes further. In a passage more remarkable for its rhetoric than for its prescience, he welcomes "the great naive Russian people" to the ranks of the democrats and actually, in his optimism and exaltation, goes so far as to say that the autocracy which "crowned the summit of Russian political life" was "not in fact Russian in origin, character, or purpose." Idealism could hardly go further than this.

This same faith in the democratic ideal animated Wilsonian diplomacy in dealing with Germany. The avowed theory of his speeches was that not the German people, but the rulers of Germany, were to blame for the war, that if the democratic forces in Germany could be liberated a new nation, to all intents and purposes, would arise. And insistence on this point of view was certainly a factor, and a very important factor, in bringing about the flight of the Kaiser and the establishment of a republic in the Reich. It may be that, in this respect, Wilson's policy was not entirely wise; it is possible to argue that a constitutional monarchy would have offered a more successful resistance to the madness of National Socialism than the republican regime could have done; but, however this may be, the moral conviction that lay behind Wilson's policy cannot be denied. To him popular government was something of a religion. And that he echoed a deep-seated popular sentiment can hardly be doubted.

In another sense, too, the notion of democracy deeply affected the policy of the war years and the making of the peace. For the democratic ideal is obviously closely connected with the principle of self-determination, and to this principle Woodrow Wilson gave pronounced allegiance. That the peace should rest upon the will of the peoples concerned was clear to him, clear to him even before the United States entered the war, set forth in some detail in the famous address of January 22, 1917. This idea was enunciated again and again after America entered the conflict; it is one of the dominating conceptions in the famous speech of the Fourteen Points. And, of course, it plays an important part in the negotiation of the treaty of peace. It was respect for this principle that made Wilson fight tenaciously French ambitions for the annexation of the Saar and that led to the setting up of an international regime in that important region, with provision for a plebiscite at the end of a fifteen-year period; it was on the basis of this principle that the President contested French designs to detach the Rhineland from Germany; it was still from the same point of view that he either actively encouraged or easily acquiesced in the various plebiscites which determined the frontiers of the Reich on the north in regard to Denmark and on the east with regard to Poland; the internationalization of Danzig was based on the same conceptions; and preoccupation with self-determination influenced the arrangements for the Italian boundary in Istria. Finally, respect for the democratic ideal led to a wholly new treatment of the problem of the backward peoples, as we have already seen. It is of course not contended that Wilson was consistent to the last degree in his attachment to principle. Few men are. The veto in the treaty on the possible union of Austria and Germany was hardly defensible; and though the question of the German population in the Sudetenland was hardly raised while the President was at Paris, he seems never to have been much troubled by the attitude of the

Czechs towards this problem. He wavered, in other words, in the pressing of his own standards of rectitude, as others have done before him and will do after him. But that democratic idealism played an important part in the negotiation of the Treaty of Versailles, and an especially important part in American diplomacy at Paris, it would be difficult to deny.

The same idealism, whether misguided or not, directed Wilsonian policy towards Soviet Russia. It was characteristic of the President that his remedy for the Russian civil war in 1919 was a conference of all factions, presumably to decide upon a peace based on democratic principle; and it is understandable that as the autocratic character of the Russian regime made itself more and more apparent the reaction of the administration was that of nonrecognition. It may perhaps be questioned whether a sound sense of political realism dictates abstention from diplomatic intercourse with governments of whose origins or principles we disapprove. It may be that it is wiser to keep the channels of communication open and hope that some breath of freedom will penetrate from the outside world. But moral reprobation is in some ways a very human form of satisfaction, and no country has carried it further in the evolution of its policy than the United States. The policy determined upon by Wilson, and enunciated by his Secretary of State Bainbridge Colby, was followed by the Harding and Coolidge administrations, and long after the other great nations of the world had established relations with the Kremlin, our own government stood aloof. It was not indeed until 1933 that the diplomatic boycott was ended.

The dislike of the Communist regime did not end with the advent of the Roosevelt administration. Anti-Communist sentiment, it is true, influenced policy to a considerably less degree in the thirties and was naturally suppressed, from motives of convenience, in the years of the war. But it was not slow to revive as soon as the struggle was over. From the pure point of view of national interest, there was really very little reason for the United States to concern itself with the character of the governments that were set up in Bulgaria and Rumania. Yet the United States made itself from the outset the defender of democracy in this part of the world and sought to prevent the transformation of these two states into satellites of the Kremlin. The case of Poland was, in many respects, similar, though here the anti-Russian feeling of American Poles rested on a broader basis than pure ideology. But a diplomacy less affected by considerations of principle might well have tried to bargain and to agree to let the Soviet government pursue its own course in Eastern Europe in exchange for a policy more considerate of American interests in Western Europe. I do not say, let it be clear, that such a policy would have succeeded. It probably would not have done so. But the fact that it was not even attempted is surely significant.

Ideological considerations have played a substantial part, also, in the American attitude towards Communist China. The question of the recognition of the Peiping government, it is true, is a complicated one, and the fact that this regime waged war against the United States and that it has consistently violated the armistice ending that war no doubt goes far to explain such an attitude. But another factor, beyond a doubt, is a deep repugnance to the brutality and violence which are so evident in the regime of Mao Tse-tung.

It is not only dictatorships of the left that have fallen under American condemnation on moral grounds. It is impossible to weigh accurately the elements which entered into the equation in fixing American hostility to Adolf Hitler. But surely among them was the brutal persecution of the Jews and the outrageous bad faith of the Third Reich in the international sphere. In the same way there existed in the forties a deep repugnance to the regime of General Franco. From the purely objective point of view, Americans might have judged the Spanish government less harshly than they did. In retrospect, whatever the sympathies of the Caudillo, it seems fairly clear that cautious neutrality was the watchword of Spanish policy, and that the chances of Spanish intervention on the side of Germany were extremely small. Yet dislike of the government at Madrid led the government of the United States to recall its ambassador in 1946 and to support the resolution in the Assembly of the United Nations which recommended such action to the members of the international body. To take another case, during the war the United States refused to deal with the Farrell regime in Argentina, and in the elections of 1946 the weight of the United States was exerted quite openly against the authoritarian elements which rallied behind Colonel Peron. It is by no means clear that such a policy was wise; it had its roots in feeling rather than in self-interest.

Another striking case of repugnance to a dictatorship of the right is to be found in the severance of relations with the Dominican Republic in 1960. The regime of Rafael Leonidas Trujillo fostered the development of American capital and sought in many ways to woo the United States. But the repulsive character of the dictator, his unbridled acquisitiveness, his intrigues against other Latin American states whose rulers he disliked, the iron character of his rule, led to a resolution of the Organization of American States looking to a rupture of diplomatic intercourse. The United

States representative supported this resolution. And the antagonism to Trujillo in the State Department over a substantial period of time is a matter of record. The repugnance was moral.

We need spend less time on the American reaction towards imperialism, since the subject has already been discussed. Yet some examples of the uneasy conscience that often goes with acquisitiveness, in the case of the United States, may be cited. Take, for example, the ill-timed attempt of President Grant to bring about the annexation of the Dominican Republic in 1870. The attempt was no doubt absurd, a kind of shoddy deal, with overtones of land speculation, with a government that could only maintain itself by a treaty with a stronger neighbor; but what is interesting is the strong moral reprobation which the enterprise aroused in the breast of Charles Sumner and the refusal of the Republican majority, in days of intense partisanship, to go along with the President. Or take again the attitude of Grover Cleveland with regard to the Hawaiian revolution of 1893. This revolution was encouraged, if not actually assisted, by the American minister at Honolulu, and it was followed by a treaty of annexation with the United States. But Cleveland sent a special commissioner to the islands, established to his own satisfaction the fact that the course of the United States had not been free from blame, and withdrew the treaty. Indeed, he went further and, with a fine gesture of moral indignation, demanded of the authorities of the islands that they restore the deposed Queen Lilioukalani to the throne. The gesture, it is true, was futile; it was met with prompt defiance. But it illustrates well enough the moralistic emphasis which sometimes intrudes itself into American diplomacy.

Another and a rather amusing illustration of American

bad conscience where acquisition is concerned is to be found in the payments the United States has been ready to make for territory acquired by the sword. For example, the treaty of Guadalupe Hidalgo, in 1848, stipulated that the Mexican government should receive the sum of $20 million for the cession of California. Perhaps, in this case, cynics would suggest that the motive for such generosity was not one of undiluted altruism but that a desire to "grease the way" for the acceptance of the treaty by Mexico was also present. But no such consideration could possibly have had a part in the 1898 treaty of Paris, when we paid $20 million for the cession of the Philippines by Spain. Another instance of this kind of action is to be found in the famous treaty of 1914 with Colombia. The Colombian government had been understandably incensed at the role of the United States in the revolution in Panama in 1903 and at the hasty recognition of the Panamanian government by Washington. The Wilson administration, coming into power in 1913, sought to allay this resentment and negotiated a treaty which contained a virtual apology for the incident of a decade before, and which stipulated a payment of $25 million to the government at Bogota. True, this treaty was delayed for some time, and the discovery of oil in Colombia may have altered the moral aspects of the problem for some senators, such as Henry Cabot Lodge of Massachusetts. Yet no such considerations prompted the original negotiation or the widespread support which the treaty obtained from the outset on the Democratic side of the Senate.

In a little different category, but illustrating again the impulse of conscience in our dealings with weaker powers, is the attitude of the United States with regard to the Boxer indemnity of 1900. The Americans had joined with the European powers in that year to relieve the legations at

Peking, besieged by Chinese revolutionists, and had, in common with the rest, demanded an indemnity from the Chinese government. But this did not sit well on the national conscience, and it was not long before the indemnity was remitted to the Chinese government, with the understanding that it should be used for the education of Chinese students in the United States.

There are many larger issues with regard to the American attitude towards imperialism that have been already treated. Domination of other peoples, as we have seen, has always created an uneasy feeling in Americans; they naturally look towards establishing the institutions of freedom wherever they go; and their natural instincts lead them to look with favor on movements of independence from foreign control wherever these movements arise.

We spoke of a third manner in which the American moral impulse expressed itself in American diplomacy, that is, in a dislike of secrecy, especially of secret deals. The general question of secret diplomacy is to be treated later. But the matter of making bargains with one power at the expense of another, a practice of which the history of Europe is full, may well be considered here. On the whole, the American record is a very good one. There are some exceptions. A case in point is the not very scrupulous attempt of Thomas Jefferson to bribe the French government into putting pressure on the satellite regime in Spain to cede the Floridas to the United States. Yet this attempt met with violent condemnation from John Randolph, until then one of Jefferson's followers, and it came to nothing. We have to come down to relatively recent times to find another episode of doubtful morality of the same general kind. The Taft-Katsura memorandum of 1905, by which the United States bound itself to the recognition of the Japanese position in Korea in exchange for a pledge to respect the independence of the Philippines, has an extremely "practical" significance. We may cite also the action of Franklin D. Roosevelt at Yalta, in pledging himself in writing to support the claims of the Soviet Union to their former privileges in Manchuria, at the expense of China and really behind the back of the government at Peking. It is true that the President was told by his military advisers that it was essential to bring the Russians into the war against Japan. It is also true that the Chinese Nationalists later accepted the arrangement. But it is significant that this "deal" was not even recorded in the archives of the State Department and that, when discovered, it met with severe reprobation from large sections of American public opinion. Speaking generally, it is fair to say that such oblique transactions have by no means been characteristic of American diplomacy.

But there is a still larger sense in which moral judgment enters into the formation of American foreign policy. We have spoken of the democratic ideal as influencing American conduct with regard to the First World War. There was more to the matter than that. The simple judgment of many Americans condemned the Central Empires in 1914 because it was believed that these empires had started the war. A more refined judgment might point to a long train of causes and to errors and provocations on both sides. But what was seen in that fateful August was that the Austro-Hungarian government had launched an attack on Serbia, and Germany an attack on Russia. And when these initial acts of aggression (as they were widely regarded) were followed by the violation of Belgian neutrality, in contemptuous disregard of solemn treaty obligations, the partiality of many citizens for the cause of the Allies was heightened. It would be foolish to deny the influence of these events on the course of American diplomacy. If Woodrow Wilson did not hold the balance even between the two sets of contestants in the mighty struggle that was unleashed, the reason was that he, like hosts of others, had made a moral judgment with regard to the war from which he could not free himself.

Equally striking is the American attitude towards both Japanese and German imperialism in the thirties. The American government, in 1931, could not sit still in the face of the Japanese conquest of Manchuria. The foreign offices of Europe were by no means so disposed to a moral judgment, and the British, in particular, hesitated to take any stand against Japan. But the United States insisted that the question be thoroughly ventilated, and though it was not ready to challenge Tokyo to armed conflict, it put forward the famous Stimson Doctrine and even secured its acceptance by the assembly of the League of Nations. By this doctrine, as is well known, the powers of the world refused to recognize any situation, treaty, or agreement brought about by means contrary to the obligations of the Kellogg Pact, that is, by acts of force. Whether such moral pillorying of another government is wise or foolish, a futile gesture or a useful clarification of the record, is beside the point. It represents very clearly the influence of an ethical ideal in the practice of diplomacy.

The same thing can be seen in later relations with Japan. When it came to the Sino-Japanese war, there was certainly a case for a policy of appeasement from the American point of view. Our trade with Japan and our investments in Japan were far greater than our trade with or our investments in China. True, the conquest of the Middle Kingdom by Nippon tended to restrict our commerce, but true, too, we would jeopardize a far more valuable commerce by war.

And, in addition, prudential considerations might well have suggested the gentle handling of Tokyo at a time when the situation was increasingly serious in Europe. The British government (of course in a far more critical situation) seemed to be acting on just such calculations when it closed the Burma Road in the spring of 1940. But none of these elements determined American policy. It was impossible for the Roosevelt administration to frame its policy in the Far East without regard to the moral revulsion felt by the American people at the Japanese invasion of China. In the conversations of 1941, the Japanese negotiators at least hinted that a way might be found to evade Japan's obligations to Germany under the treaty of alliance of September 1940, if only the United States would grant it a free hand in its ambitious designs on its great neighbor. But it would have been practically and morally impossible for the United States to take any such position, as the polls of public opinion amply attest. Indeed, the attempted modus vivendi of November 1941 broke down just because it was out of the question to tolerate the continued domination of the Tokyo government on the Asian continent. And so the country found itself involved in a two-front war from the outset, a war that might conceivably (wisely or unwisely, as you will) have been postponed.

The same sense of moral reprobation with regard to aggression showed itself in the American attitude towards Hitler. Not only dislike of totalitarian political forms but indignation at the aggressions of the National Socialist regime, not only fear of consequences but moral indignation at the methods of aggrandizement, played a part in the steadily mounting tide of feeling against the Third Reich. By the end of the thirties, too, the American people were coming to a conviction that is more and more influencing policy, the conviction that the use of force for the purposes of domination is inherently immoral and intolerable. Opinion expressed itself decisively with regard to the rape of Austria and the violent methods that preceded Munich, and rarely have more sincere moral homilies been written by a Secretary of State than those which flowed from the indignant pen of Cordell Hull in this period. It was the same when the Russians attacked Finland. There was, perhaps, something of a case for the Soviet Union, from the point of view of the protection of its own territory. But the war against the Finns was almost universally denounced in the United States. And, in the period since 1945, the steady imposition of Communist power on the satellite states, though not necessarily dangerous to American security, though hardly more, from one angle, than the consolidation of a position already attained by the victories of Russian armies in the war itself, has met with a steady stream of condemnation in this country.

But the most striking of all examples of American moralism in international affairs is to be found in the doctrine of collective security. The very root of this doctrine lies in the idea that the use of force in the settlement of international disputes is morally wrong and that the social interest requires that all states shall combine against an aggressor. Not national interest, narrowly defined, but the public peace becomes the foundation of policy. It is true that the United States declined to accept the responsibilities implicit in this point of view in the twenties and thirties, and repudiated at the polls the great leader who propounded it. But the doctrine survived, and we have heard much of it since the end of the Second World War. Consider, for example, the American action in Korea in 1950. The cold-blooded could have given many reasons why the issue raised by the invasion of South Korea might have been allowed to pass unchallenged. The government of Syngman Rhee, to judge from the elections of May 1950, had few roots in Korean opinion. The military problem presented by the giving of aid to that government was a difficult one, both because the weather conditions were peculiarly unfavorable to counteroperations against the forces of the North and because the problems of supply were peculiarly difficult. Moreover, the Americans had to fight with their backs to the sea, in a position where defeat would mean nothing less than evacuation. Finally, there was always the risk that Russia or China would intervene (as actually happened in the case of China). Yet none of these things affected the issue. The decision taken by President Truman at this time received the almost unanimous support of the nation; it was a decision based in no small degree on fundamental principles of international morality. There was, of course, an argument of another kind, and a good one, the argument that appeasement would only lead to new challenges, until an explosion was inevitable. But this does not invalidate the conclusion that a strong moral impulse influenced American action.

A still more striking case is the position taken by the American government in 1956 when the Israelis, the British, and the French invaded Egypt. The French and British were our allies; the Israelis were our friends and had many sympathizers among the Jews of the United States. On the other hand, we had no particular reason to admire the Egyptian leader, Colonel Nasser. Yet the United States sharply denounced the invasion, aligned itself in the General Assembly of the United Nations with the Soviet Union in the voting, and had a hand in bringing a halt to the whole enterprise. A less moralistic view of the matter might have led the administration either to hold its hand or, perhaps more wisely, to have offered its services as a go-between. The hurt inflicted on our relations with France and Great Britain was deep. But an austere view of American duty was what prevailed.

Still another example of American moralism in the world of today may be given. It has been impossible for the United States to accept the *fait accompli* with regard to Soviet expansion in Eastern Europe, especially Soviet aggression in Hungary. There are those who would argue that it is wise to accept accomplished facts. But this is not the attitude assumed by most Americans, nor has it been the attitude of the Truman, the Eisenhower, or (so far) the Kennedy administration.

To assert these things, be it said in conclusion, is not to fall into that kind of oversimplification which attributes to a single factor a total influence over events. It is not to say that American foreign policy is always altruistic, that it is not directed by conceptions of national interest, that it is always either in its methods or its objectives to be unqualifiedly commended. It is only to say that *ideas,* and ideas connected with certain moral preoccupations, are a factor, and a substantially important factor, in the conduct of diplomacy. And there are Americans who would add that some of the strength of the nation flows from just these facts. When men go to war, they are actuated by many motives, by mere conformity, by patriotism, by the fear of danger, by understood self-interest, but also, and not infrequently, by the belief that they are defending right and justice. And whether this belief is justified or not in the eyes of the skeptical analyst, it is one of the mainsprings of that courageous devotion which brings victory.

V

The American Attitude Towards War

I N a preceding chapter we have seen that the Americans
have, on the whole, not been an imperialist nation and
that they are not one today. But the point may suggest that
the people of the United States are a peculiarly peaceful
people, who have rarely taken up arms and only then under
the most extreme provocation. Undoubtedly, this is the
view that most Americans hold with regard to themselves.
What does the historic record reveal?

It is difficult to measure the peaceful or bellicose nature
of any people by exact standards. One might try to count
the number of wars in which a given nation had been engaged. But precisely what is a war? Should we, for example,
in the case of the United States, count the military operations that took place in the Dominican Republic and in
Haiti in the course of its intervention there? Should we
count the really very numerous Indian wars in its history,
the war in the Northwest in the 1790's, Jackson's campaign
against the Creeks, the Black Hawk war, the Seminole war,
the Sioux war, to name only the most important? And were
we to try to carry further this process of enumeration,
would we take no account of the circumstances under
which a war began, whether, that is, it was a naked war of

conquest or whether it was virtually forced upon a naturally pacific nation? It would be extremely difficult to arrive at valid conclusions by this simple process of counting, it must be admitted.

But, however we calculate it, the record is not one of undiluted peace. In 1798 we went to war with the French on the seas. From 1801 to 1805 we fought a naval war against the Barbary pirates. In 1812, only seven years later, we went to war with the British. In 1846 we went to war with Mexico. Thenceforth, insofar as international conflict was concerned, there was a full half century of peace. But in this same period, the bellicose instinct was expressed in the most prolonged and, in terms of human life, the most costly of all our wars, the internecine strife of North and South. In 1898 we went to war with Spain. After seventeen years we found ourselves involved in the First World War in Europe. Twenty-three years after the end of that struggle we were again involved. And only five years after the defeat of the Axis, our troops were engaged in Korea. Taking this record as a whole, it does not seem to be a strikingly pacific one, at least not utterly out of line with the record of other nations.

If, moreover, the balance turns in favor of the United States, it might be contended that good fortune enters into the account since, in expanding across the continent, we were generally able to accomplish our purpose without actually plundering some other established nation. We began by acquiring in the peace treaty with Great Britain an immense area west of the Alleghenies. We went on, by the greatest windfall in history, to double the area of our national domain by the fortunate acquisition of Louisiana from France; a mere caprice of Napoleon Bonaparte gave us an empire, almost in the literal sense of the word. We

84076

EMORY AND HENRY LIBRARY

were saved from direct national sin in the case of West Florida and Texas by the fortunate habit of our settlers, who moved on into territory under foreign control and then started revolutions there; and, in the case of East Florida, the unauthorized invasion of the province by Andrew Jackson made unnecessary anything but moral pressure upon the decrepit government of Spain. We might, too, have had our troubles in the Northwest. But in the middle of the nineteenth century, British ministries almost always drew back before the possibility of a serious clash with the United States, and, accordingly, by a little bluster and by a little enterprise (the movement of our settlers into part of the disputed territory), we got our way. I have very little respect for hypothetical history, and yet does it not seem probable that a nation of the vast and restless energy of the United States, had it not been favored by fortune, might well have engaged in war for the acquisition of this rich domain? One can, at least, easily imagine such a contingency.

Let us, however, return to the historical record and see precisely what it reveals as to the American national temperament, as to how Americans have shown restraint in taking up the sword, and as to the kind of motivation that has brought the American people to a clash of arms.

On the side of national restraint, there are at least two generalizations that can be made. The United States has never gone to war over an "incident." The record of the years indicates that, while a single dramatic event may, of course, intensify popular passion, there is always a train of circumstances behind the actual taking up of arms. In 1798, for example, the American people were no doubt affronted by the rough treatment accorded their representatives in Paris, when the French government attempted to extort from the delegates of the United States a forced loan and a bribe as the price of the cessation of French aggression upon American commerce at sea; but this aggression had already been going on under trying conditions for some time and had produced in this country an irritation to which the rebuff of the so-called XYZ mission only added. Again, the most irritating episode in Anglo-American relations in the troubled period of the second Jefferson and the two Madison administrations was, beyond question, the assault of the British frigate, *Leopard,* on the American war vessel, *Chesapeake;* but it was not until five years after this event that the United States took up arms. The war with Mexico, as has been said, was not produced by the Mexican crossing of the Rio Grande and the skirmish of Mexican forces with those of General Taylor. It is perhaps more difficult to rule out of account in such dogmatic fashion the sinking of the *Maine* in Havana harbor in 1898 as a factor of the first importance in engaging in hostilities with Spain. But for some time before this happened the American people were being lashed into a mood of profound indignation over Spanish misgovernment and brutality in Cuba, and into an equally profound sympathy with the struggle of the Cubans for independence. Coming down to the world wars, it is significant that the sinking of the *Lusitania,* while it provided the issue which led to the eventual entry of the United States into the struggle against Germany, preceded by nearly two years—May 7, 1915, to April 6, 1917—the actual declaration of hostilities, and that the sinking of the *Athenia,* at the beginning of the period 1939–1945, produced hardly more than a ripple on the surface of American opinion. It is dangerous, of course, to speak with dogmatism in the complex field of human affairs, but it seems correct to say, on the basis of our history, that while a dramatic incident may heighten the popular indignation that leads toward war, there must be for Americans a longer train of causes actually to produce an armed conflict. In one mood, an incident will have little or no effect whatever; in another, it may add fuel to an already rising flame; but it can never be regarded in and of itself as the explanation of an American resort to arms.

There is another generalization closely connected with this. As a rule, the American people have been rather slow to anger. The outrageous treatment of American commerce by the French which led to the explosion of 1798 began at least as early as the winter of 1796; the indignities to which American trade and the American person were subjected by Great Britain long preceded 1812; the Cuban conflict and insurrection which finally led to intervention in 1898 had begun in 1895; the aggressions of Germany to which America raised objection were, as we have just seen, of long standing in 1917; and the menace raised by Hitlerian and Japanese ambition was well recognized several years before the attack on Pearl Harbor. Even in the case of the struggle with Mexico, President Polk made what must, by the candid historian, be regarded as a bona fide effort to reach a settlement with the government at Mexico City before resorting to war. It is in a gathering irritation rather than in some sudden outburst of feeling that the basis of American action is to be found.

To say this is, of course, only to say that the action of the United States in international affairs is deeply influenced by its democratic forms. No prudent statesman in a democracy will force the issue until public opinion has been pretty clearly crystallized; he must and should wait upon its gathering force. And since it is the essence of the democratic principle that dissent can and should express itself, the integration of the people's will is bound to be a longer and more complex process than it is in a totalitarian state. We can, with caution, even go a little further and say that it is probable that the first occasion of direct challenge is not likely to cause an actual outbreak of conflict; and that, for better or worse, a democratic nation will always have a little of the water of appeasement in its blood.

In the third place, it may be said that the United States has never directly plotted aggression, in the sense that Hitler plotted it in the 1930's and the Soviet Union plotted it in 1939 against unhappy Poland. The reader may think the Mexican war an exception; but it is to be noted that Polk, on coming into office, would have accepted a settlement with Mexico which involved the fixing of the boundary at the Rio Grande but did not bring New Mexico or California under American rule. That it has been free from the acquisitive instinct in war, it would be impossible to say. An itch for territory had something to do with the War of 1812 and much to do with the war with Mexico. The "imperialist" urge was certainly present in 1898. There are new American bases in the Pacific today as a result of the war of 1941–45. But this does not mean that the American government has ever cynically started out on a career of conquest. And, as we have seen in a preceding chapter, the American people, in the main, do not relish the idea of ruling over others or take kindly to the idea of expanding their dominion by the sword.

Nor can it be said that the wars of the United States have been fought chiefly at the behest of economic interests. We have already analyzed this matter and need not repeat here what has been said. That economic forces have played a part in some of these conflicts is not to be denied. The land hunger of the West was one of these forces in 1812 and in

1846. American sugar interests in Cuba were, for the most part, in favor of intervention in 1898. Banking interests undoubtedly were strongly pro-Ally in 1917. But in the last two instances these pressures were not of central importance. They were, as we have tried to show, minor, not major, factors in shaping the American decision.

Let us now turn to the other side of the account and seek to determine what the factors are that have led in the past to a clash of arms. In the first place, it should emphatically be said that Americans have not needed to be invaded to be provoked to war. It is true that the sneak attack of the Japanese on Pearl Harbor precipitated the actual taking up of arms in 1941; but it is also clear that a dangerous tension existed in our relations with Germany and Japan when that event occurred. With the Reich we were at that moment already engaged in a quasi-war on the seas; with Japan we had already broken off commercial relations, and were giving positive aid to a Chinese government which was resisting Japanese aggression. There may be some naive people who, in judging the conflict with Mexico, still put faith in President Polk's remarkable statement, in justification of hostilities, that American blood had been shed upon American soil, but our diplomatic historians have time and again pointed out, first, that it is doubtful whether the territory on which the first clash of arms occurred was really American and, second, and more important, that Polk had made up his mind for war before the clash occurred.

In the other wars in which the United States was involved there was not anything even remotely approaching a physical assault on the domain of the United States. We can then rule out the notion that only direct attack on the national soil has been the cause of American participation in war.

In three of the six wars in which the United States has

been engaged, the immediate and avowed reason for taking up arms was the violation of American neutral rights. In 1798, at the time of the informal war with France, this was linked with the sense of insult created by the extremely cavalier treatment of our envoys, sent to Paris to secure the redress of grievances. In 1812, it was linked with a variety of other factors, the British intrigues with the Indians in the West and the hope of further expansion being among them. In 1917, it was linked with a sense of moral reprobation of the German cause and a feeling that the victory of the Reich might be dangerous to the interests of the United States. But, in every one of these instances, a significant factor (we do not say the *only* factor) was resentment at indignities suffered by the United States at sea.

There are several points of interest about this fact. In the first place, they demonstrate the fact that there is such a thing as national dignity and honor. This sentiment is not the same as that more generalized moral feeling which made Hitler and Tojo odious in 1941; it has nothing to do with consideration for the feelings of others, as did, for example, in one of its aspects, the intervention in Cuba in 1898. It is a characteristic of a somewhat different sort. In the cool calculation of national interest, in the midst of a general conflagration outside our borders, it might be argued that the best course is to keep out of trouble, risk no internal division, and make money out of the sufferings of others; this, of course, was the philosophy of the Neutrality Proclamation of 1793 and of the subsequent policy of Washington. But in practice the United States has never succeeded in maintaining this point of view; it has been goaded into war by the conduct of the belligerents. It has placed the national dignity before considerations of prudence. The fact, it must be conceded, is more important in retrospect than it is in prospect, for the old conceptions of neutrality appear today to have been eroded or abandoned. Still, there is a significance in what we have said. For, to repeat, it points to the fact that national pride is a factor in international affairs; and the Americans have demonstrated by their past that they have an ample supply of that commodity, that, though they are not roused at once, they *can* be roused by repeated assaults upon what they consider their self-esteem.

Perhaps we should go a step further. The idea of neutral rights is a *legal* conception. Far as we are from the rule of law in international affairs, the notion that there *ought* to be a rule of law is one that, historically, has been deeply cherished by Americans; it lies behind the Covenant of the League, behind the Kellogg Pact, behind the Charter of the United Nations; its existence suggests that it would be very difficult to lead the United States into a war of naked aggression. Respect for the reign of law had much to do with the American entry into Korea in 1950. It was to take up arms in behalf of legal principle that President Truman decided in June of that year to come to the aid of the South Korean government; the conception of an orderly international world was thought to be endangered.

That moral conceptions enter into the acceptance of war by the Americans is, as we have seen, equally clear. It would be futile to deny that humane feeling for the Cuban insurgents in 1898 was a large factor in producing the war with Spain; that the feeling that Germany had provoked the war of 1914 influenced American policy; that, even more, reprobation of the tyrannies, the obscenities, and the calculated aggressions of Nazism did something to goad the American people into action in 1941; that Japanese imperialism in China was, by many Americans, judged in moral terms.

Mixed with these motives, however, there has often, but not always, gone apprehension with regard to the national security, either in actually bringing about conflict or in promoting agreements with other nations out of which conflict might arise. So significant, indeed, is this that the question of national security ought to be considered in some detail.

In the informal war with France and in the War of 1812, the security interests of the United States were little involved. Certainly, the fear of actual invasion or attack had nothing to do with the inception of the brief conflict with France upon the sea. Once the issue was joined, some of the more excitable of the Federalists began to talk of a descent upon the American coasts and to agitate for larger military forces, but they made no great impression either upon Congress or upon public opinion. In the War of 1812, the country was, it is true, actually invaded. The British not only seized positions on the periphery, such as Castine, Maine, and the remote post of Michilimackinac, but they also landed a force on Chesapeake Bay, threatened Baltimore, and took and burned Washington. But, in the period preceding the struggle, none of this appears to have been foreseen. In his war message of June, President Madison in no way anticipated a direct threat to the soil of the United States.

That there were American security interests outside the national borders, however, was early perceived and clearly expressed by President Jefferson in regard to the question of New Orleans. In an oft-quoted letter to Robert Livingston, the President declared that the possession of New Orleans by France was a threat to the United States and that, if the port came into French hands, "we must marry ourselves to the British fleet and to the British nation." The instructions to Monroe on the famous mission of 1803, which was to result in the purchase of Louisiana, directed the diplomat, if his overtures for purchase met with no success in Paris, to proceed to London and there seek to bring about an alliance with Great Britain. For a moment, at any rate, Jefferson was ready to make this question a fighting issue. Eight years later the resolution of 1811, laying down the principle that the United States could not see with indifference the transfer of Florida to any other power, was a kind of definition of a security zone.

That regions so close to the borders of the United States should be regarded as involving a security interest was by no means strange. But it is something of importance that Monroe, in his message of December 2, 1823, declared the reconquest of the Spanish-American colonies to be dangerous to our *peace and safety*, language which usually conveys a threat of possible war. The President made no distinctions of geography. His declaration, in theory at any rate, covered Patagonia as well as Mexico. It was, indeed, an amazing expression of doctrine, a sweeping and questionable definition of an American sphere. So extensive a definition of American security interests, however, was in 1823 hardly likely to be accepted in practice. The Monroe administration itself drew back from implementing its famous pronouncement. President Polk, in 1845, while not expressly repudiating the language of twenty-three years before, declared that Monroe's principles applied with greatly increased force to the North American continent. And in this same administration no attempt was made to interfere with French and British action against Argentina. On the other hand, the Polk administration and its successors did not hesitate to apply the famous declaration to the regions of Central America, and in the sixties, when Napoleon III sought to set up a puppet empire in Mexico, Secretary Seward made it very clear that the United States could not tolerate such action. In 1895, at the time of the controversy over the Venezuela-British Guiana boundary, a security issue was raised, on the basis that British possession of the mouth of the Orinoco was dangerous to the United States. In none of these cases did the administration resort to actual war; it was not necessary to do so; but by the end of the century there is little doubt that the whole Caribbean area was regarded as an American security zone. As we have seen, the interventions which we have already discussed were primarily based on this fact.

It is in the twentieth century that the security thesis has undergone a portentous growth. The acquisition of the Philippines gave to the United States a stake in the Far East; what had come under American rule must be defended. This necessity was accepted with a certain reluctance. In the Washington naval treaties of 1922, the American government sought to protect its interests in the Orient by disarmament and agreed not to increase its fortifications in the Far East as the price for an agreement with Japan on naval ratios. But this experiment was doomed to failure, and by the middle thirties it was clearly recognized that the Far Pacific was, in a very real sense, an American security zone.

The change in the American attitude with regard to Europe in this same period was scarcely a less striking one. In the long and relatively peaceful era of the nineteenth century, the question of a European threat to the integrity of the United States hardly arose. The secure might of British sea power made it hardly necessary to think in any such terms. But, by the time the First World War broke out, the situation had already begun to change. There were, we repeat, many factors that played a part in American entry into the struggle. No doubt the question of neutral rights was the determining cause of our taking up arms. But there was also another way of looking at the matter, the fear that the physical integrity of the United States might be threatened by a German victory. One way of putting it (and no one put it more persuasively than did Walter Lippmann) was to assert that America could no longer be safe if the scepter of maritime supremacy passed from the British to the German people. But more than this was involved. Many distinguished Americans thought that the Reich constituted a genuine threat to the physical safety of the United States, among them President Emeritus Charles W. Eliot of Harvard University, President A. E. Alderman of the University of Virginia, Chief Justice Edward D. White of the Supreme Court, Theodore Roosevelt (who became known as the leader of the "war party"), Henry Cabot Lodge, Elihu Root, and Robert Herrick, the author of *The World Decision*. Read the publications of the National Security League (the title is suggestive enough) for the years 1914–16 and you will see that the idea of an actual physical invasion of the United States played a part in the thinking of the time. It matters very little whether the danger existed or not; security is a metaphysical as well as a physical conception. The fact that it was thought to exist is a symbol of a significant alteration in the American point of view.

At the same time there developed a significant thesis which sprang from the apprehensions aroused by the war. This was the thesis of collective security, the thesis that aggressive war was an evil to be guarded against by the mass action of mankind—in other words, that the peaceful nations of the earth must seek common means of halting an outbreak of hostilities. President Wilson had begun to think about this idea as early as the fall of 1915 (even earlier in a purely American setting); he endorsed it publicly in the spring of 1916; and, in the veiled form peculiar to such documents, it was inserted in the Democratic party platform of the same year. Nor was the matter a purely partisan one. Republicans could point out that Theodore Roosevelt's peace address at Christiania in 1910 contained the germ of the same theory, and Henry Cabot Lodge, not yet moved to another point of view by splenetic hatred of the President, put the idea forward in a speech made at Union College in 1915. When America entered the war, the idea of collective security (for this is the phrase that came to be used) was reiterated again and again in Wilson's speeches; as we know, it played a large part in the negotiations for peace at Paris and was expressed in treaty form in the Covenant of the League of Nations. That it had not been assimilated by American public opinion, however, was soon apparent. The struggle over the Treaty of Versailles was so saturated with partisan and personal animosities that it is difficult to make a stable and final judgment upon it; but it may be that, in one sense of the term, Wilson had the right of the matter in his firmly proclaimed devotion to Article 10 of the Covenant. This article contained the famous pledge "to respect and preserve against external aggression the territorial integrity and political independence of the members of the League," and this is the very essence of the collective-security idea. Reluctance to make so sweeping a commitment, which might in very truth involve the use of American troops in any part of the world, was most certainly one of the factors in the defeat of the treaty. This country was not ready for any such commitment; it did not accept either intellectually or from emotional conviction the thesis upon which the Covenant was based. The German menace having been exorcised, men again began to hope for a world in which no such far-reaching promises would be necessary for the preservation of peace.

In the twenties American notions of security for a time contracted. As we have already said, in the East an attempt was made to win Japan to peaceful courses by a pledge not to fortify Guam or the Philippines; in Europe American troops remained but a little while; the theory of the First World War seemed no longer applicable. But there came a momentous change in the later thirties. Both in national and international terms the security thesis had to be revised. In October 1937 President Roosevelt first enunciated it in cautious language that committed us to nothing; but by 1939 he had begun to sound the tocsin against the peril of German aggression in no uncertain terms. We cannot analyze here his speeches in detail. But, quite rightly, he discerned a new era in which technology had made aggression a very different matter from what it was a quarter of a century before; and in speech after speech he insisted upon the real physical danger in which the United States might stand from the aggression of Hitlerian Germany. The sense of danger was communicated to the nation, especially after Hitler's victorious march to the Atlantic and the Channel in the spring of 1940; and, for the first time in its history, America began to arm on the grand scale in time of peace. The danger from the East was also apprehended clearly; the physical security of the Philippines was certainly threatened by the onward march of Japanese arms. The issue was much more easily perceived, indeed it was much more real, than it had been in 1917, and, among the motives that led the United States into the Second World War, the sense of direct danger was definitely one of the foremost. The polls attest the fact; and so, too, does the common memory of a large body of Americans.

Once again the idea of national security soon became linked with the idea of world security, of collective security; the ideal proclaimed hardly a quarter of a century before by Woodrow Wilson was re-enunciated in the Atlantic Charter; and in 1944 began the preliminary studies which, in due course, were to lead to the conference at San Francisco and to the drafting of the Charter of the United Nations. This time, moreover, there were no hesitations in American opinion. The Charter, standing by itself, with no extraneous questions to confuse the issue, was ratified by the impressive vote of 89 to 2.

The idea of collective security in the broadest sense— that is, the idea of general international action against an aggressor nation—was supplemented by more restricted application of the same principle. In the protocols of Chapultepec and Rio De Janeiro, the American nations entered into an agreement to take common action against a violator of the peace in the New World. In 1949, the North Atlantic Pact, to which originally eleven European nations were parties and which was later subscribed to by three others, applied the same principle to Europe. After the Korean experience of 1950, the Republican administration of Eisenhower entered into a number of collective-security arrangements in Asia, with the government of Chiang Kaishek on Formosa, with the government of Syngman Rhee in South Korea, with Thailand, Pakistan, the Philippines, Australia, New Zealand, France, and Great Britain in the so-called SEATO pact, with the government of South Vietnam, with Japan by the peace treaty of 1951, and gave its blessing to the so-called Baghdad Pact, aimed at promoting peace in the Middle East. The policy of no-alliances was not only scrapped; it was reversed in the most striking fashion. The skeptic may ask whether the commitments thus entered into would be faithfully observed in the world of today; we shall revert to this question in our closing chapter. But whether observed or not, the striking extension of the principle of collective security has been one of the most interesting features of American diplomacy since the Second World War.

Have the wars in which the United States has engaged shaken the foundations of democracy? In the broad sense, the answer to this question is most certainly no. In the bloody days of its Civil War, in the midst of the titanic struggle of 1941–45, elections took place as usual. In the years preceding its entry into the Second World War, there were melancholy prophecies by the America-Firsters that if the United States took part in the struggle, popular government would not survive. Events have refuted them.

There has been a far greater tendency towards concentration of power in the federal government in America's later as compared with its earlier struggles, but there is here, I think it fair to say, a secular tendency with regard to the role of government in general. Moreover, it is to be noted that there has been a substantial relaxation of federal authority when war has come to an end.

A more serious question is that of governmental action against those who oppose a given conflict. There have certainly been instances of harsh action against dissenters. The earliest example was the Alien and Sedition Acts of 1798, which, however, lasted for only two years. Lincoln used his war powers broadly to suspend the writ of *habeas corpus* and to detain on suspicion not a few dissentients. In the Wilson administration the Espionage Acts of 1917 and

1918 dealt harshly with critics of the President's policy.

In the Second World War so complete was the unity of the nation that the question of suppressing criticism hardly arose. Nonetheless, a serious limitation on civil liberty took place, a limitation far more significant than any imposed in previous wars. Japanese living on the West coast, many of whom were citizens, were placed in camps to guard against the danger of disloyal action. The move is all the more subject to criticism since in Hawaii, where a large Japanese population existed, no such measure had to be taken and no serious problem resulted from the liberal attitude assumed.

There is also one case in which not war, but the aftermath of war, resulted in a serious assault on the rights of the citizen. The collapse of Nationalist China in 1949 and the war in Korea resulted in the proscriptive McCarran Act of 1950 against Communists and in the outbreak of witch hunting associated with the name of Senator Joseph R. McCarthy of Wisconsin. That in the operation of the McCarran Act, and in the investigations of McCarthy, much injustice was done to individuals is undeniable. Fortunately, the hysteria died down in time, and McCarthy himself was thoroughly discredited.

As to the future, it is difficult to say. The sharpness of the competition between the United States and the Communist states suggests that tolerance will be difficult. Apprehension is always easy, and it is possible to believe that in the tense world of today dissenters would receive short shrift if war came. Yet, looking at the question in the broadest way, it is fair to say that up to this time the American people have not, when the trial has come, surrendered their essential liberties or yielded to the Moloch of war the hard-won and long-practiced democratic customs which have distinguished America in the past.

VI

The American Attitude
Towards Peace

————— ·◆▶· ◀◆▶· ·◆· —————

I N the preceding essay we have attempted to analyze the
American attitude towards war. That the Americans are
capable of being roused to bellicose action is amply attested
by their history. That their notions of security have
changed, and indeed must change, with technological advance and the physical drawing together of the various
parts of the world is patent. But, looking at the record of
the past, it may still be said that Americans are not a warlike people in the proper sense of the word. They have not,
in general, glorified war; they have not desired to put their
major efforts into preparations for war; they have wished
to believe that some other method of settling international
disputes was possible; and they have been reluctant to give
to force the place which we must concede it occupies in the
scheme of international relations. The reasons for these
various emphases deserve analysis and explanation.

One very powerful influence in shaping the peace-loving
side of the American character is the extraordinary security
which the people of the United States have enjoyed during
a great part of their history. On the east, the broad Atlantic

served as a virtually insuperable barrier to any European nation which lacked a foothold in the New World. On their southern border, at the outset of their history, there was only the decrepit sovereignty of Spain, and this sovereignty was soon to be liquidated. On the west, they were momentarily threatened by the French acquisition of Louisiana which would have put a powerful nation on their flank, but the danger passed in a brief time with the cession of the province. On the north was Canada, a British possession and one which exposed them to invasion, as in the War of 1812. But relations with Great Britain, though sometimes strained, never involved armed conflict after 1814; and from the Treaty of Ghent thenceforward the peace of the border was undisturbed, so far as any threat to the United States was concerned. Indeed, the neutralization of the Great Lakes by the treaty of 1817 was a symbol of a relationship that has hardly a precedent in the international intercourse of powerful nations. Thus the Americans were physically safe in a sense that has been true of very few peoples.

This has been, in all probability, the most important, but by no means the only, element in the formation of the American attitude towards peace. The American heritage in the intellectual sphere had something to do with the matter. It has been well said that the United States was the child of the eighteenth century. The rationalistic and optimistic view of human nature which was so often characteristic of that great era, which finds itself reflected in the wisdom of Franklin and the idealism of Jefferson, played no small part in the development of the American mind. And war runs counter to any such point of view. If man is infinitely improvable and capable in time of using the power of reason to settle all his problems, so runs the argument, then the appeal to force is a denial of an essential faith. In the present imperfections of the human spirit it may have to be accepted and tolerated. But it cannot possibly be regarded as desirable or as intrinsically worthy. The dream of a peaceful world, on the basis of the assumptions just mentioned, is a dream, which in the very nature of the case must some day be clothed with reality.

The course of events in the nineteenth century may have done something to confirm Americans in this point of view. For few periods in human history, judged by relative standards, have been more peaceful. We cannot here examine the reasons for this in detail, though it seems probable that the principal explanation lies in the extraordinary economic expansion of the epoch, both through the industrial revolution and the widening of the area of settlement and trade open to the nations of Europe. But, whether this be the essence of the matter or not, it is certainly a remarkable fact that there was no war of the largest scale or of long duration in Europe between 1815 and 1914. The Crimean War, the longest and that involving the largest number of nations, was essentially local and lasted only two and a half years. The various wars of liberation, the Italian wars of 1858–59, the wars of Prussia with Austria and France, were even briefer. The Russian conflicts with Turkey were also short. On the whole, Western man had never enjoyed so great a tranquillity. In the world of the nineteenth century, then, it was natural that people like the Americans, generalizing on the facts of experience and inclined towards optimism by the progress they had made in so many ways, should come to believe that peace was a realizable ideal and should hope for its attainment.

Still another element in shaping the American point of view is to be found in the economic circumstances of

American life. The great preoccupation with material progress, immensely justified by the strides towards economic well-being taken by the American people, naturally suggested the costliness and therefore the folly of war. The dream of the "good society," of a world in which there is plenty for all, caught the American imagination and seemed incompatible with perpetual strife. Moreover, contrary to the views of our Marxist friends, the capitalist society is by no means essentially warlike. We may not go so far as Quincy Wright has gone in his monumental work, *A Study of War,* and describe it as the most pacific of all types of economic organization. But we can say, on the basis of the evidence already submitted, that the American business classes have, in general, been very far from warmongers or the allies of the more bellicose forces on the American scene. Indeed, there seems to be considerable warrant for the proposition that it is in the relatively submerged economic groups, such as the dispossessed middle class to which Adolf Hitler appealed, that the germ of virulent nationalism is more likely to be found. The dreams of the capitalist, and his theory of values, do not fit in well with a huge national debt, a regimented society, and the widespread destruction of material wealth which are a part of the war-making process.

In addition to all these things, there is a sense in which the democratic form of government is promotive of the pacific spirit. For, though democracies are capable of great excitement, though popular pressure may sometimes force a reluctant administration along the path of war, the very fact that the issue must be debated, and cannot be decided by fiat, tends to reduce the opportunities for conflict. The so-called preventive war of which the militarist mind naturally dreams is virtually incompatible with the existence of popular government. There is another restraint on action imposed by the democratic form. Those responsible for the decision for war can be retired from office, if they have misjudged sentiment or if they fall short of the objective of victory. There is in this fact, too, an influence that cannot be measured but that is certainly to be taken into account. Furthermore, the very essence of democracy is government by consent. Perhaps the best thing that can be said about the whole process of self-rule is that it substitutes agreement for force, that it assumes as a necessary foundation of policy submission to the will of the majority, once that majority has spoken, and to use the familiar cliché, that it "counts heads instead of breaking them." Closely connected with the democratic process, moreover, is the role of the courts, which offer, particularly in the United States, a refuge from the abuse of power by the majority and which lay the emphasis on orderly process for the settlement of disputes, rather than upon resort to violence. When a people is accustomed to the procedures which we have described, it is hardly likely to glorify war per se, or to indulge for long in dreams of conquest and of imperial rule.

One other force may be mentioned in connection with the pacific strain in the temper of the American people. That strain is the influence of Christianity. Here, it is true, one must proceed with caution. The great Christian churches, it must, I think, be conceded, have usually in the long run reflected the moods and the prepossessions of the societies in which they operate; they have not, in essence, determined these moods and prepossessions. Yet, at the same time, the churches preserve a tradition of conduct which is utterly opposed to the ruthless use of force. Their ministers have expressed themselves again and again in this sense. The peace societies, so numerous in the United States, have derived no little of their strength from religious sources. The anti-imperialist movement of the turn of the century sprang from the same origins. It is impossible to deny the significance of this factor in the general composition of the American mind.

But perhaps, in proceeding so far, we have blandly asserted something that the reader desires to see proved, that is, that there is in the American temperament a very real and grave concern for the interests of peace and a desire to see these interests prevail. The history of the United States amply demonstrates the proposition which we have so far taken for granted, and any analysis of American foreign policy will make this clear.

There are few nations where the teaching of history is less nationalistic than it is in the United States. Read the best historical works on the American Revolution and you will find genuine consideration given to the British point of view. American youth of today are not taught that there was but one side to the very struggle that gave the nation birth. Obviously, if we accept the famous dictum that "Die Weltgeschichte ist das Weltgericht," the Americans were right and the British wrong. Obviously, most Americans are glad to be Americans. But that there were two ways of looking at the great constitutional controversy of 1765–75 would now be clearly understood by most educated Americans, just as it would be understood that there was a case for the South in the Civil War of the 1860's. The ideal of balanced judgment has deeply influenced teaching as to both these fundamental conflicts.

What is still more interesting is America's judgment on its past wars. It is a striking fact that, when a kind of historical perspective has been established, many Americans tend to think of former struggles in rather objective terms, to deplore them as foolish, or even to display a bad conscience with regard to them.

Take, for example, the War of 1812. It has been argued that this second conflict with Britain was unwise and unnecessary. It has been pointed out that a war for neutral rights is, in its essence, rather futile. You cannot vindicate such rights by fighting. You can only increase the dangers to which your own commerce is exposed. And you may end, as the United States did in 1814, without securing the slightest recognition of the principles for which the government has been contending. Or take another critical viewpoint as to our second struggle with Britain. The Madison administration, it is said, was entirely unprepared for the effective waging of the struggle. It undertook to lead the nation into war at the cost of national unity, and the bitter opposition to the war in New England jeopardized the fabric of the union and even led to talk of secession. The whole business was a mistake; it would have been better if the nation had never taken up arms.

Such are two interpretations of this war. But one of the most eminent students of that struggle has gone further. J. W. Pratt, a scholar of great distinction, has put forward the thesis that the motives of the United States in 1812 were, in part at least, imperialistic and that the desire of the West for Canada and of the South for Florida resulted in a coalition of these two sections to enlarge the boundaries of the Union by means of an armed conflict. It is true that this thesis has been subjected to a good deal of criticism since it was first enunciated. But the significant fact for us here lies in its *being* enunciated. American historians feel no compulsion to defend past national actions or to justify past wars in nationalistic terms.

We can see the same thing in connection with every one

of America's periods of belligerency. Take, for example, the war with Mexico. Here the critical view has been again and again put forward and is, indeed, contemporary with the conflict itself. The action of President Polk, we have more than once been told, was highly provocative; he instructed General Taylor in the winter of 1846 to occupy territory which was in dispute between the United States and Mexico; Taylor himself behaved badly in blockading the Mexicans across the Rio Grande River at Matamoras; and the Mexicans were thus goaded into armed action. Polk's real objective was conquest; the war ended in the acquisition of Mexican territory. It was a true war of aggression and should be so regarded.

There is a similar interpretation with regard to the war of 1898, given popular currency in that brilliant work of Walter Millis, *The Martial Spirit*. According to this view, the Spanish government had virtually conceded the essential American demands in April; it had agreed to suspend the reconcentration policy in Cuba, a policy which had shocked American opinion; and it had indicated its willingness to grant an armistice to the Cuban insurgents. President McKinley, however, gave little emphasis to these concessions in his message to Congress, and in the prevailing temper of American public opinion that body lost little time in declaring war. Thus, through the weakness of an American President (so runs the argument or the implication), the country was launched into an unnecessary conflict.

In the case of the First World War, also, there is a school of historians who have held that the conflict could and should have been avoided. At the distance of about a decade from the struggle, American revisionists made themselves heard with a new theory of the events of 1917–18.

Matter-of-fact citizens had for the most part assumed that Germany's challenge to the United States on the high seas had been the cause of the United States' taking up arms. But the case was restated in very different terms. The policy of the Wilson administration (so it was contended) was, from the first, very far from what it should have been. British propaganda directed American opinion; the administration never honestly carried out a policy of neutrality. Moreover, it was influenced by a desire to extend American trade. The munitions traffic produced profits that gave the United States a stake in the cause of the Allies; so, too, did Allied loans; and these economic forces afforded much of the true explanation for the policy pursued; a policy, be it said, confused and tortuous, and never candidly explained.

The Second World War very soon became the subject of criticism, and from the pen of one of the most eminent and respected of American scholars. The late Charles A. Beard in *America and the Coming of the War* laid down the thesis that President Roosevelt committed himself to a policy of peace in the electoral campaign of 1940; but in 1941 he so shaped events that war became virtually inevitable. In respect to Germany, he secured from Congress the so-called Lend-Lease enactment under the pretense that this measure of assistance to Great Britain would prevent war; he then extended the action taken to patrols and then to convoys at sea; he instructed the American navy to take action which almost inevitably would provoke the Germans to war; he misrepresented as an act of defense the famous episode of the destroyer *Greer*, which at the time it was attacked by a German submarine was following that submarine and reporting its position to British vessels and air patrols; he sought a showdown at the very time that he was professing to avoid it, and the showdown came. In his relations with Japan he was no less ingenious: he fixed terms for an understanding that could not be accepted; he put aside the offer of a personal conference with Prince Konoye, the Japanese minister, in the summer and early fall of 1940; he declined to accept proposals for a modus vivendi; by his action he encouraged the Japanese to the "sneak attack" on Pearl Harbor, which indeed was more or less foreseen in advance. Moreover, the war into which he led the United States was a futility; for while it destroyed the power of Hitler and of militarist Japan, it left a new and more dangerous totalitarian state in a position of supreme power. It brought not peace, but a situation more dangerous and troubled than ever.

I do not, be it understood, endorse any one of the views expressed above. Indeed, there is much to be said against many of them, and, in principle, it is dangerous business for the historian to assert too dogmatically what must be only hypothesis and to pretend, let us say, to *know* that war would have been avoided in 1898 if McKinley had acted somewhat differently, or to *know* the Second World War would have ended in the exhaustion of both Germany and Russia if we had abstained from interference. But the point is not there. The existence of this guilt complex, as it seems fair to call it, in the minds of many historians and its acceptance by many Americans is a matter of very great significance when it comes to analyzing the American character. It indicates very clearly indeed how little prone are citizens of the United States to glorify conflict.

There is another way of illustrating the devotion of the Americans to some ideal other than that of sheer power in international affairs. Speaking comparatively (and how else can one speak with any real illumination?), the United States has made great use of the processes of peaceable adjustment of international disputes. No doubt, the very fact that the country did not build up great armies and navies itself explains why it sought recourse to arbitral settlements; where no great physical power existed, the expediency of turning to other methods for the settlement of international disputes was perhaps necessary. Yet the insistence on these peaceful processes is nonetheless significant; and it has a very long past in American diplomacy. The Jay Treaty provided for a considerable number of commissions to decide disputed questions: the Maine boundary, the British debts, neutral claims. There were further arbitrations in the Treaty of Ghent in 1814. Many irritating disputes of a minor character involving our relations with Britain were settled by mixed commissions in 1853. A really important controversy, and one that aroused national feeling to a very considerable degree, the question of the *Alabama* claims, was settled by arbitration in 1872. At the same time, the question of the San Juan water boundary was successfully solved by an arbitral tribunal. The decade of the nineties saw the settlement of the Venezuela-Guiana boundary and of the Alaskan seal fisheries by the same procedure, and in 1903 the Alaska boundary was submitted to peaceful adjustment. And the complicated problem of the northeast fisheries, which had long resisted diplomatic agreement, was finally successfully adjudicated in 1910. Nor must it be thought that arbitration of disputes down to 1914 was confined to our controversies with a single country. Of sixty-eight disputes solved by this method only twenty-two were with Great Britain. Furthermore, the United States became a party to multilateral agreements for the pacific settlement of international controversies in the Hague Conventions of 1899 and 1907, and in 1907 sponsored vigorously the drafting of a convention for the compulsory arbitration of disputes arising out of contract debts. In addition to all this, in the Wilson administration, a new device for the maintenance of peace was brought into being to supplement the use of arbitration. The famous Bryan treaties, by which the signatory nations agreed to submit to investigation and conciliation any controversy which could not be settled by the ordinary processes of diplomacy, represented a very considerable advance over previous practice, even though they did not satisfactorily provide a mode of procedure in the case of a continuing injury (like the submarine warfare). It is also worthy of note that these treaties were most of them accepted almost without dissent by the Senate of the United States. Finally, a whole series of agreements for conciliation and adjustment of disputes have been worked out with the republics of Latin America, through the machinery of the Pan-American Union. And, in our own time, by its adhesion to the Charter of the United Nations, and its acceptance of the World Court created under that Charter, the country has again demonstrated the importance that it attaches to the peaceful settlement of international controversies.

In the catalogue of American efforts to deal with the problem of international relations in a pacific context, there are other expedients that call for comment. It is interesting to observe the faith that has existed among many people in this country in economic coercion as a substitute for war. The colonies had tried this method with some success in the early days of the great controversy with Great Britain. Thomas Jefferson applied it on a far more ambitious scale in the embargo of 1807–09, and though the experiment failed, the idea of some form of commercial pressure persisted in the legislation of 1809, and in the famous Macon Bill Number 2 of 1810. These examples, particularly the embargo, have a peculiar significance, for they were adopted at a time when the fashionable doctrine was one of limited powers for the federal government and when, nonetheless, the most sweeping exercise of authority had to be employed to apply the idea of economic coercion. Something more than twenty years later, though the Whigs made great play with regard to the bellicosity of the Jackson administration in the pressing of the French spoliation claims, what Old Hickory really proposed was nothing more than measures of commercial retaliation. In the twentieth century, too, the idea that economic pressure might be a satisfactory substitute for war was more than once brought forward. If one reads with care the central article of the Covenant of the League of Nations with respect to coercion, Article 16, one will find that it is drafted in very precise terms with regard to the use of the commercial boycott and concomitant measures, but that it is very vague with regard to the use of physical force. It seems quite obvious that the authors of the Covenant hoped and believed that the one might make unnecessary the use of the other. In the middle thirties, when the League attempted to apply economic sanctions against Italy, the attitude of the United States was sympathetic, if somewhat equivocal. The severance of commercial relations with Japan in the summer of 1941 represented a desperate effort to check the course of Japanese expansion without war.

It is very doubtful indeed whether economic pressure is a substitute for war. It may be true, as Henry Adams pointed out many years ago, that the law of physics can be applied to politics, that force can be converted only into its equivalent force, and that, if economic coercion is to do the work of war, it must extend over a longer time the development of an equivalent energy, a time so long as to make the whole experiment of doubtful wisdom and precarious advantage. Certainly the policy of Jefferson was a failure, and the boycott against Japan brought war nearer rather than thrusting it into the distance. The important consideration lies in the fact that Americans have wished to believe that there was some way of bringing a recalcitrant nation to terms which did not involve the use of overwhelming physical power.

The Americans have also believed in the possible efficacy of moral power. The best example of their faith in this regard, a faith which we must reluctantly concede to have been somewhat excessive, was the Kellogg Pact of 1928. As is well known, by that pact, which was promoted by the United States, the powers of the world almost without exception pledged themselves not to resort to war as an instrument of national policy and to settle all disputes arising between them by peaceful means. To expect that such a pledge would be kept seems to us in the climate of opinion of 1962 to be almost fantastic. But even though we must concede that the Kellogg Pact was not brilliantly successful in preserving the peace of the world, we must not brush it aside as of no significance. Whatever its practical inefficacy, it illustrated in graphic fashion the devotion of the United States to the cause of peace. Naive it may have been; but what other people would have been so simple-mindedly idealistic as to believe that the tranquillity of the world could be based upon promises alone?

In a preceding chapter we have discussed the protocols of Montevideo and Buenos Aires. It is not necessary to consider them again. It is only necessary to remind the reader that here again the implicit assumption is that disputes between nations can be, must be, settled by means other than armed conflict. Probe the diplomatic history of the United

States in any detail and one will find plenty of evidence of a dislike of force and a repugnance to war. Finally, in connection with the peace spirit, we must examine the American attitude toward the military establishment and the whole question of armament.

For the greater part of its history, the United States has maintained very small forces indeed in relation to its population, its resources, or its far-flung domain. Take, first, the question of the army. At the outset of the War of 1812, the total land forces of the United States amounted to about 12,000 men, this for a country of some seven million. In 1846, when we went to war with Mexico, the total had actually fallen to 7,640 men. The vast armies raised in the Civil War were speedily dissolved, and by 1890, the regular army had shrunk again to a mere 27,000 men. It was scarcely larger at the time of the outbreak of the war with Spain. Then came what, by the comparative point of view, was a substantial rise. The imperial commitments undertaken by the United States, and perhaps the growing nationalism of the Roosevelt era, resulted in a substantial increase in the military establishment which stood in 1912 at 213,000, more than half of whom were in the National Guard. But this was infinitesimal as compared with almost any other great nation and represented less than a fourth of one percent of the total population. The world war, though it resulted in the raising of more than three and a half million men, left no permanent mark upon the fortunes of the establishment. By 1935, the total number of enlisted men was only 137,000, actually less than it had been twenty-three years before. By 1940, on the verge of American entry into the Second World War, it had mounted to only 269,000. Such forces were infinitesimal compared with the armies of Europe.

During this whole period the Americans showed a distinct dislike for compulsory military service. The early American conflicts were fought with volunteers. In the Civil War, a struggle for national existence, the draft was adopted only in 1863, and then applied in such a way as to make it very far from universal in practice. It was not until 1917 that the country came to the acceptance, in an unqualified way, of the principle of conscription in time of war, and with peace the old reliance on volunteer forces was revived. In the Second World War, the government moved more rapidly, and legislation of a sweeping character was adopted in the summer of 1940, more than a year before American involvement. But the extension of this legislation for a term of two years passed by a single vote in the House of Representatives in 1941, despite an increasingly serious international situation. Nor does the United States have universal military training today. It depends for the most part upon volunteers, with the draft as a distinctly secondary measure of recruitment.

What has been the situation with regard to the navy? The United States began its career as a nation without any navy at all. Though there was some progress in developing a substantial force in the decades that followed, and though the small American navy gave a good account of itself in the War of 1812, it was not until the Civil War that a really powerful navy came into being. With the end of the war, the country reverted to something like complete impotence. By the mid-eighties the tide had turned again, but as late as 1905 the total enlisted personnel was only 15,000. The Roosevelt era saw a considerable expansion, and a considerable increase in effectiveness, and the events of the First World War brought about a very large naval program. Furthermore, the nationalism of the war period produced a demand for equality with Britain on the seas, a demand which most certainly implied a very drastic departure from the standards of the nineteenth century. Yet the period in which this demand was made was also the period in which the idea of reduction of armaments was most earnestly advocated and most effectively applied in practice. By the treaty of 1922, to which Great Britain, France, Italy, and Japan were signatories, along with the United States, at the instance and under the leadership of the American government, capital ships and aircraft carriers were limited and a substantial number of ships were scrapped, in the interest of arms reduction. Eight years later at London the three great naval powers entered into an agreement for the limitation of all types of naval vessels. In addition to all this, by the agreement made in the earlier of these treaties not to fortify Guam and the Philippines, the country virtually abdicated so far as the use of force in the Orient was concerned. Perhaps no great nation, able to outbuild virtually every other power, has ever made gestures so magnanimous in the interests of peace.

But what of the situation in the last decade and a half? Has the temper of the United States decisively changed? Have the events of the world war, and the secular rivalry of the United States and the Soviet Union, altered the American psychology? Have the peace forces in the United States been compelled to give ground to the warmongers? What has been the temper of the American people in the more recent epoch?

It is undeniable that the United States now maintains a far larger military establishment than at any previous time. Its forces in 1959 amounted to almost two and a half million, a large figure, even though substantially below that of the Soviet Union or the Chinese People's Republic. Nor is it possible to gainsay the fact that new and terrible weapons of war have been forged and that there exists today a formidable competition in nuclear armaments. Is this the responsibility of Washington?

The American government was, of course, the first government to come into the possession of the atomic bomb, and it used that bomb to bring the war with the Japanese to an end. What then? Did it use its power to terrorize the rest of the world? It did not. On the contrary, in 1946, it brought forward an elaborate plan for the internationalization of nuclear weapons, the so-called Acheson-Lilienthal-Baruch Plan. We cannot discuss the details of that plan here. But it seems fair to say that the Russian government, instead of working for a viable agreement, deliberately frustrated such an agreement and that it preferred competition in nuclear armaments to understanding. Naive people have been and are confused by the ingenious Russian propaganda on this whole question. The Kremlin puts forward high-sounding proposals with regard to these matters which becloud and muddy the issue. In the world in which we live, the observance of an arms agreement of any kind can only be guaranteed by a workable system of inspection. Such a system the Russians have never, as of this date, been willing to accept, while the American government has constantly declared its willingness to do so. Preponderant American opinion has been strongly in favor of understanding on this matter.

One may, indeed, go further. With regard to the use of atomic weapons, American opinion is in flux. But there is certainly a considerable body of thought that would maintain that such weapons ought never be used except in retaliation, and naive though it be to talk in this way (thus diluting or nullifying the deterrent involved in the possession of nuclear arms), many Americans, including a former President of the United States, persist in doing so.

It is not, I think, a mere pretense to maintain that the armaments of the United States today are essentially defensive in character. It is probably as true as it has ever been that this country could not enter into a preventive war. Proposals for such a solution of international tension, when made by conventional militarists, are still given short shrift by American public opinion. There has not been any attempt on the part of the United States since 1945 to extend the area of its power by measures of physical coercion. The foreign policy of the American government makes constant appeal to the desire of the American people for peace and seeks to justify every move as a guarantee of of peace. True, the tone of public debate has changed. Where once the American people refused to look in the face the possibility of aggression, such a contingency is now openly and frankly discussed. But it is by no means the case that the movement for an increase in the country's effective military power is without opposition or that some of the historic elements in making up the pacific spirit of the nation have ceased to operate. On the contrary, there is still a rather romantic attitude towards the process of international negotiation, still a remarkable faith that somehow or other if only the two sides can talk to one another some kind of agreement will be reached. This was never better indicated than in the strong demand for a meeting at the Summit which sent President Eisenhower to Geneva in 1955 and again in 1960—without very positive results.

The same pacific tendency is shown in the prevailing American attitude towards the United Nations. While the Russians have again and again resorted to the veto in the Security Council, while many of their actions have tended to diminish the prestige of that organization, while they have leveled attacks on the Secretary General and seem disposed to reduce the operations of the great international agency to impotence, the American government has taken a positive view of its functions at almost every turn. Indeed, the whole idea, first of the League and second of the United Nations, owes much to the initiative of the United States.

In thus tracing the American attitude towards peace, we must not of course exaggerate. Nations, like individuals, are ambivalent. The instinct to violence exists in all of us. Looking back on the history of the United States, we have seen that the American people have been by no means uniformly pacific. They have engaged in wars which were wars of conquest, or which have been frequently so adjudged; they define their own security in terms more extensive geographically and in terms of greater military preparedness than ever before; they have entered into commitments such as have never before been made. And they have shown, also, certain oscillations in mood. To this question of oscillation in mood we shall turn in the next chapter.

VII

A Cyclical Theory of American Foreign Policy

————◄•►————

I N the two preceding chapters we have examined the
American attitude towards peace and war. The pacific
and the bellicose instinct, we have seen, are both represented in the history of the United States, both expressed
in the temperament of the American people. And this suggests a question of some import: is there a rhythm in the
foreign policy of the United States? Does this rhythm
suggest any significant generalizations with regard to
American action in the future?

Our answer to the first of these two questions, as will be
made apparent in the course of this essay, is yes. There is
a distinct pattern to be traced in connection with America's
wars. But with regard to the second of our two inquiries,
the answer cannot be so clear. This is the case for a signally
important reason. During a large part of its history the
United States has moved in an orbit of its own. Its emergence from isolation came, on the broadest construction,
only some fifty years ago. In the period between the two
world wars, it was still, in many respects, able to act independently of the European powers in a world which

continued to retain many of the characteristic features of the era before 1914. But today it is one of two great powers whose ideological rivalry and conflicting desires with regard to the future dominate the whole international scene. The mood of the United States in the future is bound to be determined in substantial degree by the mood of the masters of the Kremlin. And how, indeed, are we to measure that? What do we really know of the men who determine Russian policy? We cannot find a satisfactory answer to this question in the Russian past, for tsarist despotism was one thing and a despotism based on a militant social dogma is another. In a country where public opinion is manufactured from above, where it is formed by a few men who stand at the levers of control, it is impossible to make any rational calculation. We shall have more to say of this whole matter later. For the present, however, it is sufficient to remark that the present situation is so extraordinary, indeed so unprecedented, that it would be rash indeed to try to predict the future on the basis of historical analogy.

Nonetheless, a cyclical theory of American policy will have value from several points of view. On the one hand, it may help us to understand the past more clearly—a gain in itself. In the second place, it may serve to exorcise the romantic, and not particularly useful, superstition that man is automatically advancing along the road to permanent peace and that Americans are, in the very foundations of their national character, leading this advance. And, in the third place, assuming that international relations may, after a period of tension, assume a more normal character, it may shed a little light—only a little, but still a little—on the relationship between the mood of war and particular elements in the national life.

The task of analysis with which we are confronted is, however, a somewhat difficult one. It is not easy to divide the history of a nation into periods clearly marked out from one another. The past is a seamless web, and there is something artificial about the process of dividing it into separate pieces of cloth, some to be marked red, some blue, or what you will. Moreover, in distinguishing the periods of peace from the periods of bellicosity, it is difficult sometimes to fix the date where one ends and the other begins. But we ought not on this account to be deterred from attempting generalization. History serves us best when we seek to make some kind of useful pattern out of its myriad facts. We must not *force* the pattern, of course. But we may hope to find one that does no violence to scholarship and has a positive value. Let us, then, see what we can make of the story of American diplomacy.

The foreign policy of the United States as a nation begins in 1789. And the general temper of the American people for the first two decades of our history may, in general, be described as pacific. The reaction of the nation to the French Revolutionary wars was, as we have seen before, in favor of neutrality, and this neutrality was really endorsed by the friends of France no less than by the friends of Great Britain. The policy of accommodation with Great Britain, represented by the Jay Treaty, was, on the whole, accepted by the nation, as demonstrated by the ratification of the treaty itself and by the election of John Adams in 1796. Nor, I think, do the events of 1798–1800 show a very pronounced spirit of bellicosity. It is true, under the influence of the French violations of neutrality at sea and of the publication of the XYZ papers, grossly insulting to the national dignity, that an informal war with the French republic was begun in 1798. But who-

ever examines carefully the records of the time must take
account of several significant facts that make this informal
war totally unlike the larger struggles in which the American people were to be engaged. First, it was virtually a
partisan enterprise, and nothing more. An analysis of the
votes in Congress demonstrates that it never commanded
the united support of the American people. Second, it was
accepted only reluctantly by the Adams administration
itself, which seized upon the first opportunity to bring it
to an end. Third, it was not possible for the Federalist
enragés to turn it into a war of conquest (as some of them
probably desired) or to secure any substantial support for
the building up of the army. It is, therefore, perhaps fair
to treat the French war as a very brief interlude in a period
the dominant note of which was pacific rather than bellicose. We must take note of it, but we must also, I think,
distinguish it from later conflicts.

The general temper of the American people in the first
decade of the nineteenth century was certainly not exactly
militant. Here, again, we cannot forget that there was a
little war, the war with the Barbary pirates. But if we
examine the larger scene, we get a different perspective.
When Thomas Jefferson, consummate politician that he
was, declared that "peace is our passion," he doubtless reflected the general set of public opinion. Even in the face
of gross violations of American rights on the seas, the
United States was for a time not stirred to war. On the
contrary, as we have already seen, it put its faith in economic coercion as a substitute for war, and the embargo
and the nonintercourse acts were the expression of this
faith.

But in the year 1810 there came a change. The elections
of that year brought into Congress a group of men who

were bent on rousing the country to positive action. On the whole, they dominated the political scene, and they, far more than the President of the United States, were responsible for the War of 1812. Though the struggle itself was entered into reluctantly, though there was much factious and sectional opposition, there was also evident a very distinct stirring of the national pride and an attitude very different from that of 1798. Certainly in its total effect on the American people, the war was evidence of a growing nationalism and of a distinct shift from the mood that had preceded it.

Moreover, the war left behind many evidences of an aroused national spirit. One of the generalizations which we may make with assurance with regard to the effect of armed conflict on the American people, perhaps on most peoples, is that it leaves behind as a rule a mood of self-assertion. Most historians would agree that the conflict of 1812 had very distinct results in fortifying the national consciousness of the United States. Diplomatic historians might well point to a spirit very different from that of the Jeffersonian era in the field of foreign affairs. No one can read the story of John Quincy Adams' administration of the State Department without discovering there an extremely vigorous, if not militant, attitude. Read, for example, the famous note to Erving of November 28, 1818, in which the Secretary defends the invasion of Florida by Andrew Jackson and Old Hickory's cavalier putting to death of two British traders, Arbuthnot and Ambrister. Examine the conversations of Adams with Stratford Canning. Reflect upon the extreme boldness, and the self-confident spirit, expressed in the noncolonization principle, or in the declaration of December 2, 1823, with regard to Latin America. All these things demonstrate that the

United States of the postwar period was very different in temper from what it had been at the beginning of the nineteenth century.

Yet, by the time the Monroe administrations had finished their course, the pendulum had swung towards a quieter and less flamboyant mood. There was much partisan politics behind the opposition to the despatch of American agents to Panama in 1826. But partisanship, as we shall see, usually capitalizes on something real in the public feeling. And the cautious note of Adams' own deliverances in this period, and of Clay's despatches, contrasts strongly with the almost defiant tone of the message of 1823. Moreover, strange as it may appear, the administration of Andrew Jackson was notable, on the whole, for a very moderate diplomacy. There was, it is true, the flurry over the French spoliation claims. But the policy of the President in this matter was strongly denounced by many of the Whigs, and Jackson himself was thinking not of war but of much more limited measures. On the whole, Old Hickory disappointed his critics by conducting American foreign affairs in what was, speaking generally, a very restrained spirit. And his attitude was prolonged into the administration of Martin Van Buren and indeed into the early days of the administration of John Tyler, as indicated by the Webster-Ashburton Treaty.

But now a new note asserts itself. The Texas and Oregon questions arouse attention. And the election of 1844 is remarkable for a new outburst of perfervid nationalism and for the ringing cry of "fifty-four forty or fight." The national temper had certainly undergone a change, and though the dispute with Great Britain was peacefully settled, the Polk administration led the United States into the war with Mexico. The vote in Congress on the declaration of war was a very decided one, and the pride of the American people in the military exploits of their leaders was reflected in the victory of a military hero in the election of 1848.

Once again, the mood of war was followed by a wave of national self-assertion. The Whig administration, it is true, was disposed, on the whole, to be cautious. But Secretary Webster found himself obliged to join in the general hullabaloo which attended the visit of Kossuth to the United States, and to answer in one of the most florid of diplomatic notes the protest of the Austrian government at the reception accorded the hero of Hungarian independence. As for the Pierce and Buchanan administrations, they were remarkable, especially the first-named, for exhibitions of bumptiousness which have hardly a parallel in American experience. The mission of the tempestuous Soulé to Spain, the shameless recognition of the filibusterer William Walker as president of Nicaragua, the tone assumed towards Great Britain with regard to Central America, all attest the strength of American nationalism, a sentiment perhaps exaggerated at this time by the consciousness of division at home.

Moreover, in this case, the national mood of combativeness did not evaporate, as had been the case in due course after the War of 1812. On the contrary, it expressed itself in a great civil conflict, in the bloodiest of all struggles in the Western world (the civil war in Paraguay excepted) between 1815 and 1914. This conflict resulted, as had previous ones, in a new fillip to the national spirit.

There was a strongly nationalistic note in the diplomacy of the late sixties. There was a vigorous popular demand for driving the French out of Mexico and substantial resentment against Great Britain, which was shown in the almost unanimous rejection of the so-called Johnson-Clarendon convention for the settlement of claims many of which had arisen from the war. But this time the reaction came quite speedily; and a mood of comparative quietude seemed to establish itself. On the whole, the diplomacy of the seventies and the eighties was not adventurous; there were, at least, no great foreign crises. In the nineties, however, the scene changes. The Hawaiian revolution of 1893, which might easily have led to the annexation of new territory, brought about no such result, it is true, and Grover Cleveland perhaps had the nation behind him in withdrawing the treaty of annexation from the Senate; but Cleveland himself in 1895, in his famous Venezuelan message, issued a challenge to Great Britain which has been quite generally regarded as an expression of a newly aroused and militant nationalism. By 1896 the Republican Party, in its platform, was calling for intervention in Cuba, and the bellicose mood of the country was clearly demonstrated in the opening years of the McKinley administration. The country went to war with a light heart in 1898, and with a unanimity that had marked none of its previous conflicts.

The United States emerged from the episode of 1898 in a mood of self-confident and robust nationalism. The new national temper was exemplified in Theodore Roosevelt, and though it is only fair to say that the Rough Rider was far more cautious in action than in utterance, the general tone of his administration was saturated with a new spirit, with a strong feeling that America must play a great part on the stage of the world. The temper of the times is well demonstrated in the movement towards a larger navy, in the agitation of the Japanese school question, in the despatch of the fleet around the world, and in the cool reception accorded the arbitration treaties of the Roosevelt administration by the Senate of the United States. But with the next administration, the pendulum swung back; by comparison with his predecessor, Taft was an extremely restrained executive in the field of foreign affairs, avoiding war with Mexico, which might have come with the turmoil of the Mexican revolution, and watching with comparative indifference the rising tide of national rivalry in Europe. Moreover, in continuing the Roosevelt policy in the Caribbean, Taft met with very considerable opposition from the Democrats, and the same thing was true of his attempt to strike out on a new line in the Far East. Finally, the arbitration treaties with Great Britain and France (though they were rejected by the Senate) expressed a pacific spirit that was, in many quarters, widely acclaimed.

The relatively conservative mood of the Taft administration was carried over into the first years of Wilson's Presidency. The country, on the whole, approved of Wilson's restraint in dealing with Mexico, and it certainly was behind him when he proclaimed American neutrality at the outbreak of the First World War. The first reaction to the European conflict was distinctly pacific; the Congress elected in 1912, and whose sessions were, of course, not terminated until March 1915, did little to prepare for possible American entry into the struggle; and the Wilson administration itself, confronted with the submarine issue, resorted to note writing and not to war. As late as 1916, the strength of the peace sentiment was reflected in the great vote cast for President Wilson.

Once again the tide turned. There were signs of rising discontent with the peace policy as early as 1915; by 1916 the preparedness movement had made substantial headway, and when, in 1917, Germany sharply challenged the American point of view with regard to the undersea warfare, the country entered with reluctance, perhaps, but with resolution as well, into the struggle in Europe. Indeed, the Republicans in this period were capitalizing on the change in public sentiment by denouncing the weakness and flabbiness of the Wilson administration, and Theodore Roosevelt was hurling his sarcasms at the President with the knowledge that many persons would agree with him.

The war of 1917 was followed by an upsurge of nationalism. True, the Washington Arms Conference represents an attempt to deal with a great international question by conference and agreement. But a different temper is evident in the struggle over the League of Nations and in the anti-Bolshevik hysteria of 1920–21. Tariff bars were raised, restrictive measures were enacted with regard to immigration, and, in connection with this latter subject, Congress, in a blatant and wholly unjustified nationalism, refused to apply the quota system to immigration from Japan. The tone of the Coolidge administration in its early dealings with Mexico reflected something of the same spirit, as did the break-down of the Geneva naval conference in 1927.

Yet, by this date, the tide had distinctly begun to turn. In 1927, the Senate was voting unanimously for the arbitration of our disputes with Mexico, and by 1928 was giving its almost unanimous adherence to the Kellogg Pact. The Great Depression did not alter the picture in any essential degree. The Hoover administration drew back from any really effective measures to check the advance of the Japanese in Manchuria, and the first Roosevelt years were years chiefly distinguished by the end of the Roosevelt corollary to the Monroe Doctrine and by a most conciliatory policy towards Latin America. The country wanted no foreign adventure of any kind, and this fact it clearly demonstrated in the neutrality legislation that was forced upon a reluctant administration. The predominant sentiment of the country was distinctly nonadventurous on the whole, until well into the second administration of FDR.

And now, once again, under the influence of events in the Orient and in Europe, the mood changed. The President reflected this change as early as October 1937, in the famous quarantine speech; and he actually stimulated a more militant attitude as early as the winter of 1939. The country moved on towards a greater and greater degree of involvement as the Second World War dragged out its length, and even had it not been for Pearl Harbor, it seems probable that war would have come towards the end of 1941 or perhaps shortly thereafter.

Victory in 1945 brought, if not actual bellicosity, a new wave of nationalism. The foreign-policy objectives of the United States were conceived in terms far more extensive than ever before. The government, in dealing with conquered Japan, arrogated to itself an almost exclusive role, to the chagrin of both Russia and Great Britain; it interested itself in the affairs of Iran; it sought to bolster up the Chinese Nationalists; it responded to the challenge involved in the North Korean invasion of South Korea; it developed a web of alliances in both Europe and Asia. And the various commitments made between 1949 and 1954 are in existence today.

So much, then, for our historical review. The question now comes as to what is to be learned from it. Before we answer this, let us set down the calendar of events in the form which it has taken as a result of our analysis:

1789–1810. On the whole, a period in which the pacific spirit dominated.

1810–1814. Rising bellicosity and war.
1814–1823. Postwar nationalism.
1823–1844. A period of relatively pacific feeling.
1844–1848. Rising bellicosity and war.
1848–1861. Postwar nationalism.
1861–1865. Civil conflict.
1865–1870. Postwar nationalism.
1870–1895. A period of relatively pacific feeling.
1895–1898. Rising bellicosity and war.
1898–1909. Postwar nationalism.
1909–1915. A period of relatively pacific feeling.
1915–1919. Rising bellicosity and war.
1919–1927. Postwar nationalism.
1927–1937. A period of relatively pacific feeling.
1937–1945. Rising bellicosity and war.
Since 1945. Postwar nationalism.

The first question, we may ask, is whether any conclusion is to be drawn as to the length of these various periods: the period of peace, the period of rising nationalism that precedes war, the period of nationalism that follows war. On the whole, it will be observed, the periods of pacific feeling are longer than any other. As we have analyzed them, they are respectively 21 years, 29 years, 28 years, 8 years, and 10 years. This sheds some light, no doubt, on the temperament of the American people, so far as the past is concerned. But I do not think it gives us much guidance for the future. In particular, I should not wish to try to strike any average, and draw conclusions from that average. I do not think it would be wise to take these four periods and draw from them the deduction that the peace mood would be likely to last for nineteen years when once it had begun to show itself. History rarely works in patterns as neat as this, and it would not be prudent to put any trust in such mathematical conclusions. It is, in my judgment, more important to note that the nationalistic feeling stimulated by war tends to die down. The periods of postwar nationalism are, until 1945 at any rate, 9 years, 13 years, 5 years, 9 years, 8 years, and 9 years. On the whole, it will be observed, they are shorter than the periods of pacific feeling, and this fact may be significant. It tends to bear out the general proposition, already discussed at length, that there is a strong pacific strain in the American people; and it tends to suggest, too, that, given half a chance, this spirit will in due course express itself after a certain period of postwar nationalism. One might even argue from the data that any alteration in Russian policy today, in the direction of peace and conciliation, would be likely to be met by a similar reaction in the United States.

Is there anything else to be learned from the calendar which we have constructed? It is just possible that there is. If we note carefully the rise of belligerent feeling, I think we shall find that it seems to coincide with recovery from economic disturbance. Thus, the War of 1812 came after the commercial upturn which followed the abandonment of the disastrous policy of the embargo; the Mexican War came after the years of depression, 1837–42, had been succeeded by a period of improvement; the Spanish-American War came after the return of prosperity following on the disastrous depression of 1893; the entry into the First World War came after the minor economic decline of the Wilson administration's first years had been followed by war prosperity; the entry into the Second World War came after the bad years 1937–38, when a very substantial recovery had taken place. Are these facts significant?

Again we must proceed with caution. It is worth while

calling attention to an interesting article which appeared in *Economic History* in 1937, written by A. L. Macfie of the University of Glasgow. Taking the unemployment figures of the trade unions and the unemployment insurance scheme in Great Britain, and applying them to the periods 1851–72 and 1893–1914, the author of this article points out that no European war broke out in a period of profound depression, but all of them in periods of growing prosperity, and that all are connected with the "unnatural heats" of an excessive expansion. He also points out that the wars of the nineteenth century occurred in a period of rising prices, whereas the periods 1820–49 and 1874–96, in which prices were falling, were years of peace. He points out still further that it is in long periods of prosperity that the forces seem to germinate that bring about international explosions. If we seek to apply these generalizations to the history of the United States, we cannot accept them unqualifiedly. We cannot say that an unnatural expansion had taken place in the United States in the years just preceding any of the wars in which this country was engaged. But we can say, on the other hand, that Macfie's generalizations in part bear out the analysis which we have just made. Depressions, in the case of this country as in the case of Europe, are not themselves the periods in which wars break out. On the contrary, recovery periods, whether healthy or otherwise, seem to bring with them substantial risks. It may be that as the public mood becomes more confident, as "economic bumptiousness" takes hold, to use Macfie's expression, there is a tendency for this same buoyant mood to translate itself into a more aggressive foreign policy.

Is there anything here on which to go in the practical sense? Do any of these admittedly imperfect and partial generalizations suggest a way in which to avoid the dangers of war? It would not be wise to try to apply such tentative conclusions dogmatically or too strictly. But there is perhaps one thing that might be said: if changes in the economic mood, as it might be called, tend to generate changes in the political mood, then it is possible that, if we iron out the oscillations in the economy, we shall at the same time be tending towards a more peaceful era. And because this idea is so intriguing and suggestive, without claiming for it anything like finality, it may be worth while to examine it in some detail. The question is one which belongs more to the economist than the historian; yet it is one which the historian may usefully seek to answer.

In Europe, as one soon learns from contact with European leftists, there is a strong tendency to think of the American economy in terms of 1929. Europeans of the left look forward with considerable pleasure to a future economic collapse in this country; the more moderate leftists sometimes indulge in the view that America is an economic body of death; and even those who are friendly to us look forward to the future course of our economic life with apprehension. The idea of bigger and better depressions has an undoubted influence, in other words, upon some segments of European public opinion.

Now, historically speaking, it is not to be denied that the United States has suffered from serious economic crises. Without pausing to discuss the question whether such crises are endemic in a capitalist world, there are obviously certain reasons why in the past they have played a substantial part in American economic life. In the first place, the Americans are a mercurial people. The volatility of American opinion is a factor not to be left out of account in assessing the working of our economic system. Whereas the "British phlegm" produces one kind of reaction towards the operation of the business machine, the hearty optimism of Americans, often an optimism that outruns the facts, produces another. This temperamental bias, moreover, has been combined with a strong speculative instinct that springs from the historical development of American society. In our early period of development great fortunes were to be made through a rise in the value of real estate; and the violent depression of 1837 was closely connected with the reckless buying of land. In 1873 the phenomenal expansion of the railroads touched off another wave of speculation; and in the 1920's the stock market, unregulated as it was, stimulated the avidity of Americans and rose to unprecedented and wholly unjustifiable heights. The violent swings of the pendulum, moreover, were accentuated by the strongly individualistic spirit of the American people and their dislike for or, perhaps one might say, their indifference to public controls. In particular, the credit system of the country was subjected to very little regulation throughout a large part of its history. These various factors explain much; but in the Great Depression of 1929 they assumed an unprecedented character. The farmers of the country had unduly expanded their holdings in the period of the war; their relative situation at its close was much deteriorated by the high tariffs which raised the cost of manufactured goods, while the market for agricultural products tended to contract. The rise in industrial profits in the twenties was unaccompanied by any corresponding increase in real wages. The stock market, entirely unregulated by public authority, rose to dizzy heights. The crash, when it came, was therefore without a parallel in American history. Stock values diminished, at the depth of the depression, by more than 80 percent, wholesale prices dropped one third, employment by 40 percent, farm income 57 percent, exports and imports 70 percent, payrolls 60 percent. No wonder that a catastrophe on this scale inevitably communicated its effects to Europe and produced there, in due course, an economic decline of great proportions, one which immensely stimulated the growth of political discontent and paved the way for the sensational rise of Hitler to power.

But will the course of history repeat itself? Will the United States in due time go through another 1929? Of course, there is no absolute answer to this question. A cynic has said that all there is to be learned from history is that men learn nothing from history, and, without accepting this view of human nature, it would still be possible to agree that human beings do not always profit from experience by any means. Yet the impact of 1929 on the public mind was tremendous, and, in the perspective of thirty years, it seems possible to say that it ushered in, in this country, what was hardly less than a peaceful political revolution. That the way has been found to achieve a depression-proof economic order no one but the rashest optimist would be likely to suggest. But that the character of our economy and the drift of economic thought suggest different developments from those of the twenties would seem to be reasonably clear.

What are some of the factors that make for a relatively stable economy today? First, there might be mentioned the enormous governmental spending, which is at the present time consuming in the neighborhood of a fifth of the national income and which is sustained by an arms program without a parallel in our history. Such spending is likely to be less subject to fluctuation, and especially to drastic reduction, than the spending of private industry, and it operates therefore as a kind of stabilizing force. In the second place, a whole variety of measures have been taken to sustain buying power among consumers: the placing of props under farm prices, the development of unemployment insurance and pensions, the emphasis placed on public relief, the building up of backlogs of public works to balance a decline in private employment. In the third place, machinery is now at hand (one cannot be sure it will be courageously and wisely used) to prevent undue inflation; for example, the control of the stock market, the control of installment buying and of credit. So far as we have yet gone, moreover, since the war years, there are some signs, not to be taken as conclusive but certainly interesting, that the mood of the American public itself has undergone a very substantial change. Farm indebtedness, which increased in the First World War from $3 to $8 billion, actually declined in the Second. There is, even today in the midst of great prosperity, no dangerous speculative activity in the stock market. The policy of high wages, stimulated by the growth of the trade-union movement, has taken hold and operates to distribute the national income somewhat differently, perhaps in a more healthy manner, than in the 1920's. There is a wider recognition than ever before of the importance of international trade and of the fact that the development of such trade is incompatible with a high tariff policy. And there is an unprecedented technological development which increases productivity and which, though not without its dangers, is favorable to economic advance.

Now it is not to be supposed that all these factors add up to an economy which will never suffer from recessions, or which will not have to face serious problems. Depressions are, in no small measure, a reaction from excessive speculative activity. It is impossible to be sure that no such activity will occur in the future. But certainly it may be said with confidence that the conditions of today do not parallel those of thirty-three years ago. Similarly, it is to be expected that any severe reaction would be followed by prompt government measures of reflation. One does not have to believe blindly in the efficacy of such measures; but that they would operate to prevent such a dramatic collapse as that of 1929 seems likely. I do not believe there are many economists who would not maintain that the business machine in the United States is in a healthier condition than it was and that the chances of genuine catastrophe are much less. The danger of the future lies not so much in deflation as in an uncontrolled inflation. But of this latter peril there are not at the moment many signs, and there is no reason to allow fear to influence our judgment of the future.

It is not the business of the historian, however, to prophesy; and it is necessary to end this chapter with no more than cautious and tentative generalizations. What I have been trying to say is substantially this: that there has been a rhythm in the American public mood with regard to foreign affairs; that this rhythm *may* have a connection with the movements of the business cycle; that there seems to be some evidence that the bellicose spirit is fostered by the buoyant confidence of a mood of economic recovery after a substantial downswing; and that, if the economy of a given country becomes more stable, the effects of this stability may be seen in a more moderate foreign policy. It would be foolish to go beyond these speculative comments; but it would be foolish also to deny their possible suggestiveness. Those who work to moderate the swings of the economic pendulum may well be working for world peace as well.

On the other hand, what we do not know, and cannot

know, is whether such factors are really controlling and not incidental. Still less can we measure with any degree of accuracy the applicability of any such conceptions as those just mentioned to the course of Russian policy. It would be rash, indeed, to conclude that, because the Soviet leaders have, through centralized planning and totalitarian control, immensely diminished the risks of an economic collapse, they have also created a peace psychology in the Russian people more powerful than the will of their governors. The major question of our time is just this question of the relations of the Western world, and particularly of the United States, with the Soviet Union, and in this relationship there are many factors which have to do with elements in human life other than the economic. To some of these factors we must later turn.

VIII

The Executive and American
Foreign Policy

———◆·◄◉►·◆———

O NE of the largest philosophic problems with which historians must deal is that of the influence of the individual, as measured against the influence of the mass. Is
the course of events largely determined by individual per-
sonalities situated at controlling points in the society? Or is
it largely determined by the great tides of human feeling
and emotion that spring from the body politic as a whole?
What is the interrelation of the political leader and his
constituency? These are questions that deeply concern
the student of foreign policy.

In our discussion of the moralistic influence on American
diplomacy we sought to show how great popular prepossessions and assumptions got themselves translated into action, how, in other words, mass judgment or mass feeling
influenced policy. But we must not exaggerate the role that
can be played by such feeling. For the conduct of foreign
affairs is a day-to-day business. There are decisions to be
made currently for which there is no clear guide in public
opinion, even in the most democratically governed state,
for matters indeed on which the materials for a judgment,

for assessment by the general public, are simply not at hand. Under any political system vast powers must be concentrated in the executive branch of the government, so far as diplomacy is concerned. For the United States this means, in the first instance, the President, who takes the ultimate responsibility and who, if he be particularly interested in foreign affairs, will play a highly important personal role; it means, in the second instance, the Secretary of State, the principal adviser of the President, and the department under him; it means other executive agencies which play a part in the determination of policy, such as the National Security Council, the Central Intelligence Agency, and the Department of Defense.

We must in this essay examine the role of each of these agencies, and we must, of course, give the central importance to the President himself. His, we repeat, is the ultimate responsibility and the ultimate authority; on his wisdom and judgment the nation must, in no small degree, rely. In him, under our constitutional forms, is concentrated a degree of power which we do not always realize.

The great power of the President, as far as foreign affairs are concerned, was early indicated in the pages of the *Federalist*. John Jay saw and described clearly the immense advantages that the chief executive has in such matters over the members of the national legislature. Though the power to declare war is withheld from him under the Constitution, though the treaty-making power is shared with the Senate, it is still true that the Presidency by its very nature is of vast importance on the international scene. First of all, as Jay discerned, an immense advantage lies in the unity of the office. It is obviously easier for one man to make up his mind than for a group of men to do so; in a legislative body the integration of opinion is a laborious and unwieldy process; but a single executive head ought to be, in the nature of the case, capable of prompt and decisive action. In the second place, Jay pointed out, the President has sources of information superior to those of the national legislature. The diplomatic correspondence of the representatives of the United States all over the world is at his disposal, whereas the members of the House and Senate must depend oftentimes upon more casual sources of information, or upon what he chooses to communicate to them. When they question the correctness of his judgment, they run a serious risk. Thus, in the summer of 1939, it was possible for Senator Borah, in conference with the President and Secretary Hull, to challenge their judgment as to the probability of war, but his confident assertion that he knew better than they did was made to look a little ridiculous before many months had passed. Senator Borah was a member of the Committee on Foreign Relations and was, doubtless, in a better position than an ordinary member of the Senate to assess the course of events; but even a member of this august committee is not likely to have the ample information which is provided to a President of the United States. Jay discerned a third source of strength in the office of the Presidency, in what he called the capacity for secrecy and dispatch. The conduct of foreign affairs, as we have said, is after all a day-to-day business; decisions have to be taken with great speed, and they are not always broadcast to the world at the time that they are made. They become public, not infrequently, only after a considerable lapse of time, and when it is impossible (and of this more anon) for Congress to exert over the action of the executive that supervision which would take the control of foreign policy out of his hands. In addition to these advantages, the President possesses a fourth, which was not emphasized by Jay but which is obviously of the first importance. He is, under our form of government, the only person who can speak authoritatively for the whole nation. The congressmen represent their districts, and sometimes not much more; the senators represent their states, and sometimes, fortunately, a good deal more; but the President speaks for the whole people. To no one else will the mass of men listen with the same respect; and rightly, for he comes close, in the field of foreign affairs, to embodying the national sovereignty. The apparatus by which he keeps the masses informed have, of course, become more and more institutionalized, and serve to extend his power still further: his meetings with the press are carried all over the nation; and when he speaks over the radio or is seen on the television screen, he will be heard, not by hundreds of thousands, but by millions. No one who lived through the period of the thirties will be disposed to underestimate the immense influence which Franklin D. Roosevelt wielded through the press and radio; and even a President far less well adapted to these publicity devices is likely to be listened to with an attention vouchsafed to no other public official.

In addition to all this, the President, though he is in many respects confined by the laws, has very substantial inherent powers in the field of foreign affairs. Early in the history of the government, in the second Washington administration, it was established that the power of recognition of a new regime resided in the chief executive. Whether Edmond Genêt, the representative of the new French republic, would or would not be received was determined by the President himself. And so it has been from that time forward. Nor is the act of recognition a merely ceremonial matter, or one the giving or withholding of which is determined by fixed rules. There is here a very important discretionary power, one which may deeply affect the actual course of policy. When, for example, Woodrow Wilson decided, on his accession to office in 1913, that he would not recognize the unscrupulous soldier who, at the cost of the life of his predecessor, had made himself master of Mexico, the President determined the whole course of our policy towards that republic and set in motion forces that were of great significance. Indeed, the success of the social revolution which took place in Mexico in this period might have been much more doubtful if Wilson had acted otherwise. The decision of successive administrations, in the period of the twenties, to abstain from recognition of Soviet Russia was a fact of considerable political significance. And the recognition of the government in the Kremlin by Franklin Roosevelt in 1933 was, again, a measure with substantial diplomatic consequences.

Traditionally, too (and here again the precedents were set in the second Washington administration), the President has the right to fix the course of the United States when war breaks out between other nations. The first President issued on April 22, 1793, the first proclamation of neutrality, and, though there were those, some of them eminent men, who caviled at the time, the issuance of such proclamations has been undertaken by many succeeding chief executives. In a sense, this kind of decision is less important than recognition; it merely registers an existing situation, for the most part. But the *enforcement* of neutrality is another matter. The conscientious discharge of neutral obligation, or, as in 1940 and 1941, the exercise of a marked partiality for one belligerent over the other, may well fall within the limits of the Presidential prerogative. We shall have more to say of this later.

More important than either of these matters is the fact

that, as our constitutional forms have developed, the President *negotiates* independently of the legislative body (of the Senate, that is), though the Senate must approve all treaties. This was not, apparently, the intent of the framers of the Constitution. It was expected by the founding fathers that the Senate would be a kind of Crown Council and that the executive would freely consult with it on matters of foreign policy. The episode that nipped in the bud any development along this line is well known to us through the pages of Senator Maclay's diary. General Washington, so Maclay tells us, appeared in the Senate with an Indian treaty on August 22, 1789. No doubt he expected prompt action on the draft proposal but "the business labored with the Senate" and after a little a motion was made that the papers communicated be referred to a committee. The President then "started up in a violent fret" with the exclamation, "This defeats every purpose of my coming here," and finally withdrew "with sullen dignity." Though a few days later there was a new conference with the Senate, the session of August 22 may be thought of as having determined the general principle that the chief executive communicates with the Senate in writing on treaty matters and refers to them only completed agreements, not draft agreements in process of negotiation. The rare exceptions to this general principle, such as President Polk's advance consultation with the Senate on the expediency of the Oregon treaty of 1846, only emphasize the ordinary practice.

Now Senator Maclay and his colleagues, in 1789, were doubtless influenced by a distrust of executive power and by the fear that the President might overawe the Senate. Unwittingly, however, they were abdicating what might have been an important function. For the right to pass on a diplomatic compact when completed, though important, is never so extensive as the right to participate in the drafting of it. The power to negotiate which now rests exclusively in the President's hands means that he can, in a sense, confront the Senate with a *fait accompli*. It does not mean, of course, that he can afford to take no account of senatorial opinion, or that he will not be wise to get some advance information as to the temper of that body. But, as we shall see when we come to examine the role of the upper house in more detail, the great majority of treaties are ratified without amendment, and in the form in which they have been presented. The major determinations of foreign policy, in other words, are made by the executive.

There are many ways, moreover, in which the President's control over negotiations can be exercised without close supervision. Very early in the course of our governmental history, for example, the executive insisted upon the right to withhold information from the legislative body. When the House of Representatives in 1796 was debating an appropriation measure connected with the implementation of the Jay Treaty, it called upon General Washington for the papers in the case. The answer which Washington gave was to the effect that it was not in the public interest to communicate such materials, and the House was obliged to rest content with this answer. The precedent then established, moreover, was followed in case after case and would be recognized as valid even today. While, no doubt, the power to negotiate in secret is less extensive than it was at the end of the eighteenth century, it still remains true that the conduct of diplomacy still depends upon innumerable private exchanges, some of these at the very highest level, and that the right to carry on such exchanges is an important weapon in the Presidential armory.

The implementation of this right, moreover, has been extended by the growth of a remarkable practice which again goes back to the early days of the government. That is the right of the President to use special agents who report only to him and not to the State Department. Washington used Gouverneur Morris in this way as early as 1791. Henry Wriston, in *Executive Agents in American Foreign Relations*, has prepared for us a formidable catalogue of similar personal representatives of the President from that day to the 1920's. The most striking examples are, of course, relatively recent. The role which Colonel Edward M. House played in the Wilson administration is well known. On at least one occasion, in the famous memorandum of February 22, 1916, House sought to commit the President to entry into the world war on prearranged terms; on another he acted as the emissary of the President in the negotiations of the armistice of 1918. In the 1920's Norman Davis often played an important part in negotiations having to do with the League of Nations and the reduction of armaments. In the period of the Second World War, Harry Hopkins acted again and again as the special emissary of the President, and he performed the same function for Truman in the spring of 1945. Nor, be it observed from what has already been said, did executive agents always perform merely exploratory functions. As early as 1832 an executive agent signed a treaty with Turkey, and the name of Colonel House appears on the armistice agreement of November 11, 1918.

From time to time the appointment by the President of such personal representatives has been challenged. The very fact that the agents do not require confirmation by the Senate is a sore point. But the challenge has never been successful; the practice has never for long been interrupted; and it is today thoroughly well entrenched. In fact, public opinion, on the whole, seems to approve of it; Americans often express a naive faith in the man-to-man negotiations of which the special agent is a kind of expression.

The power of the President to negotiate is supplemented by the power actually to conclude agreements with foreign powers *without* the consent of the Senate. Treaties, as is well known, require that consent, but there is another type of understanding, the executive agreement, which does not. Some of these agreements may be made under the direction and authority of Congress. For example, the President, under the various reciprocal-trade-agreement acts, has been authorized to make compacts with other nations for lowering tariff duties. Other agreements may be entered into to implement a treaty. The North Atlantic Pact, for example, has given rise to many such understandings, as have some of our other defense treaties. The third, and most important, type may be entered into by the exercise of what can only be described as the Presidential prerogative. Thus, when President Theodore Roosevelt desired to establish customs control over the Dominican Republic, and found himself thwarted by the Senate of the United States, he signed an accord with the Dominican government which put the system of control into operation by executive action alone. A still more striking illustration of the use of the Presidential power in this regard is the famous bases-destroyer deal with Great Britain in September 1940. By this agreement the President turned over fifty destroyers, described as "over-age," to Great Britain and received in return the right to erect American fortifications and installations on various British island territories, extending from Newfoundland on the north to Bermuda in the center and Trinidad in the south. It would be difficult to imagine a more audacious use of the power of the President, yet the criticism of the action taken was extraordinarily mild, and in April 1941 Roosevelt applied the same technique by signing with the Danish minister in Washington an agreement for the occupation of Greenland.

The number of executive agreements of all kinds has grown with time and in the twentieth century has actually exceeded the number of treaties. The extent of the power of the President remains undefined, and a serious attack on his powers was launched in the first years of the Eisenhower administration. But the attack failed, and we are where we were in 1953. It seems likely that future Presidents will find occasion to use their full power, as Roosevelt did. If they do so, they are not likely to be challenged. It is true, most public policies require money for their execution, and Congress, when it disliked the consequences of Presidential action, might conceivably withhold funds; but to do so would involve a repudiation of the chief executive in the face of the world and would not be lightly attempted. Impeachment would be a still more drastic remedy, and one hardly likely to succeed in view of the fact that conviction requires a two-thirds vote in the Senate of the United States. The power to conclude executive agreements has, so far in our history, never really drawn down on the head of the President a storm of criticism, and this very circumstance underlines the fact that there exists in the Presidential office a vast residual power which is capable of very wide extension.

Akin to the power to negotiate executive agreements is the power to make important statements of policy which, though not theoretically binding on the legislative body or on the nation, may very well commit the country to a given course of action. These statements may be unilateral on the part of the President, or they may be bilateral or multilateral. To take the most striking example of the first type, President Monroe, in his famous message of December 2, 1823, declared that any attempt on the part of European powers to intervene by force of arms in Latin America for the restoration of the dominion of Spain would be "dangerous to our peace and safety," and in the same message he declared that the "American continents by the free and independent condition which they have assumed and maintained, are henceforth not to be considered as subjects for future colonization by any European power." With regard to neither of these statements had Monroe in any way consulted the national legislature; the first had been discussed at length in the cabinet; the second had been adopted, so far as we know, at the suggestion of the Secretary of State without prolonged discussion of any kind; both enunciated policies which might have the most far-reaching consequences. But what Monroe did in 1823 was never the subject of any very vigorous opposition, and succeeding Presidents have not hesitated, of course, to reaffirm the principles which he laid down. In theory, it would be possible to repudiate such sweeping declarations of policy; in practice, the nation has often been committed by the pronouncements of its chief executive. And so, indeed, it is likely to be in the future.

Just as there are unilateral pronouncements by the executive, so, too, there may be bilateral or multilateral pronouncements. Thus the Root-Takahira agreement of 1908 fixed the relations of the United States and Japan and, according to some of the commentators, recognized the special interests of the Japanese in Manchuria. The Lansing-Ishii agreement of 1917 was an agreement of the same type, going so far as to describe Japanese interests in China as "paramount." But the most remarkable case of a declaration in which other powers concurred is the Declaration of Washington of January 1, 1942. By this document, signed as it was by the authority of the President and never submitted to the Senate, the nations concerned agreed to wage war together against the German Reich and to make no peace until Hitler was beaten, and then only concurrently and not separately. In other words, by this declaration, President Roosevelt came very near to doing—perhaps he did do—what had never before been attempted in the history of the nation under the Constitution, and what had been done only once at any time in the history of the United States (on Feburary 6, 1778); he virtually contracted an alliance, and this without the consent of any legislative body and indeed almost without a voice raised in criticism. No episode could emphasize more strikingly the power vested in the President of the United States.

But we have not even yet reached an end. For the chief executive possesses still another source of wide authority in the field of foreign affairs. As Commander-in-Chief of the Army and Navy he may in many ways control the course of our foreign relations and determine in practice major questions of war and peace. Thomas Jefferson, for example, determined to put an end to the practice of paying tributes to the notorious pirates of the Barbary states; he despatched American naval vessels to chastise them and to all intents and purposes waged war against the Tripolitanians, a war which was finally concluded by a treaty. In 1844, when the treaty for the annexation of Texas was under discussion, President Tyler concentrated troops on the border and ships of war in the Gulf of Mexico, of course with the intention of overawing the Mexicans, who had not yet recognized the independence of their former province. President Theodore Roosevelt established a military government in Cuba in 1906. In 1917 President Wilson, having failed, through a filibuster in the Senate, to secure authority to arm the merchant ships of the United States against German submarines, exercised this authority on his own initiative. In 1940 and 1941 President Roosevelt stretched his authority over the armed forces to the uttermost, establishing patrols over the Atlantic and, after the occupation of Iceland in 1941, sending convoys as far as Iceland. Such measures did not bring war, but they were, of course, acts of provocation; and when, in September of 1941, a German submarine understandably resented being followed and fired on an American destroyer, the President directed that all U-boats be shot on sight, a step which could hardly be described otherwise than as a direct challenge to Hitler.

Since then, we have had still further illustrations of the power of the President to use the armed forces of the United States, without having first asked Congress for a declaration of war. It was on his own initiative that President Truman sent American forces into the Korean War in June 1950; it was again on his initiative that he reinforced the American military establishment in Europe in 1951. President Eisenhower authorized the use of American naval forces in the Formosa Straits in 1955 and 1957, and ordered a landing in Lebanon in 1958 at the request of the Lebanese government. Though on the first and second of these occasions there was some criticism in Congress, the right of the President to act has never been forthrightly challenged by the legislative body. And it is well that this is so. For in the kind of world we live in today, the instant use of force may at some time be necessary, without any wait for the slow processes of congressional debate.

Flowing, too, from the President's power as Commander-in-Chief is the power to make military agreements which may commit the nation in no small degree. The peace protocol of August 12, 1898, for example, by which the Spanish-American War was terminated, called for the evacuation by Spain not only of Cuba (to whose liberation the United States was pledged), but also of Puerto Rico and Guam, and for the capitulation of Manila. Thus, President McKinley deeply committed the nation to some degree of expansion when it came to the negotiation of the treaty of peace, although, it is true, the final disposition of the Philippines was reserved. Still more important was the armistice agreement of November 11, 1918. By this agreement not only the Germans but the Allies accepted the Fourteen Points, enunciated by President Wilson in his speech of January 8, 1918, as a proper basis of peace. The signatories were thus pledged to certain broadly defined territorial readjustments, to a specific definition of reparations, and to the acceptance of the principle of a League of Nations. In the same way, the agreements made in 1944 committed the faith of the United States. To all intents and purposes, the fixing of the line between the Russian and Western occupation forces in Germany determined the future fate of a large part of Europe, while the agreement with the Japanese made it certain that Japan would evolve as a constitutional monarchy under the nominal rule of its emperor. The decisions taken in all these cases by the President could not be and were not overthrown in the ensuing period.

The list of powers of the President of the United States, as far as foreign relations is concerned, is thus seen to be a very formidable one. At first blush, it would seem as if it involved a very serious danger to democratic principle; an external observer of our constitutional system, or, indeed, a conservative American, might well raise the question as to whether there ought not to be some way of curtailing such enormous authority. But the answer to this question, of course, ought to be given on practical rather than theoretical grounds; in other words, it ought to be based on the way in which the Presidents have actually conducted the foreign affairs of the nation.

Before we embark upon any such analysis, however, there is one major generalization upon which we ought to fix our especial attention, and that is the high probability, in such a democracy as the United States, of the President's being a politician of long experience. Occasionally, it is true, a man comes to the highest office in the land without very much of a political career behind him. Grover Cleveland had served one year as sheriff of Erie County, one year in the Buffalo mayoralty, and two years in the governorship before he attained the Presidency. Woodrow Wilson had only his two years as governor of New Jersey from which to learn, at first hand, the Presidential game. Taylor, Grant, and Eisenhower had had no experience in politics. But these cases are very decidedly the exceptions. The first six Presidents of the United States all had long careers in politics. So, too, had Van Buren, Polk, Buchanan, and many others. In the twentieth century, the same thing in general was true, though the experience of William Howard Taft and Herbert Hoover was wholly on the administrative side. What this means is clear. Speaking generally, our chief executives have been sensitive to the public opinion of the nation and have been anxious to conform to it. Not many of them would deserve the sarcasm that Uncle Joe Cannon directed against McKinley that his ear was so close to the ground that it was full of grasshoppers. But most of them, in the nature of the case, are anxious, and honorably anxious, to interpret the public will. It is not merely that personal ambition and party interest dictate such a course. The matter cuts deeper. Deference to public opinion, faith in the public judgment, are a part of the democratic process as it is understood and practiced in America. Few Presidents of the United States have failed to understand this and to be guided by it. The danger that the President will act autocratically, and arbitrarily, is therefore very much less than one might suppose. If the power he exercises is in theory very great, this power in practice is limited by the sentiment of the nation.

And how have the Presidents exercised their power? Have they, for example, led the nation into war, war for which it was unprepared or about which it was divided dangerously in opinion? I do not think that the answer to this question can, in general, be given in the affirmative. In the War of 1812, for example, it was not President Madison who played the principal role. The war sentiment began to make itself felt in the congressional elections of 1810, and in the period that followed Congress was more bellicose, on the whole, than the executive. Certainly it was not a strong-willed and warlike President who led us into the second war with Britain. Nor was it the chief executive who shaped the course towards war in 1898. President McKinley was one of the most pacific of men. He was propelled towards war, even more clearly than Madison in 1812, by the public opinion of the nation. In the brief French war of 1798–1800 the impetus to vigorous action certainly came as much from Congress as from the executive.

In two other cases, in both the world wars, the influence of the Presidents in shaping the issues that finally brought us into the struggle is undeniable. But when Woodrow Wilson took, in the winter of 1915, the stand against submarine warfare which finally resulted in a severance of relations with Germany and in armed conflict, he was, in no sense, acting covertly or arbitrarily or without regard to public opinion. While that opinion is not always easy to measure, I think it may be said that the votes and discussion in Congress, as well as an examination of the newspaper press, indicate that the executive was interpreting a widespread, probably a majority, sentiment. The attacks of the opposition were for the most part, especially in the Presidential campaign of 1916, not directed to demonstrating that the President had been unwise in raising the submarine issue, but to showing that he had been weak in carrying it out. When the actual break came in 1917, it was not a divided, but a united, country that stood behind Woodrow Wilson.

More clearly still, Franklin D. Roosevelt, in the policies which he pursued in the years 1939–1941, and in his undoubted leadership during those years, was reflecting the public opinion of the nation. The polls demonstrate this fact beyond a peradventure of a doubt, and so, too, do the votes in Congress on the repeal of the arms embargo in 1939, on universal military service in 1940, on Lend-Lease in 1941. While there was at times, it must be confessed, a certain deviousness in the attitude of the President, while some of the steps which he took represented a very bold construction of the Presidential power, he cannot be said to have led the American people in a direction in which, without him, they would not have wished to go, or to have precipitated a struggle which they were anxious to avoid. This, I know, is a large subject, and one that will perhaps seem open to debate. But let those who doubt review the period objectively and I believe that they will find that the majority of the American people wished Hitler and Tojo to be defeated, that they were ready to assist the democracies against the German peril and sided with China against Japan, that, while they would of course have preferred to see justice triumph without their active intervention, they were ready to go as far as necessary in order to assure the defeat of the militarists.

In two instances the role of the President was more important, perhaps decisive: in the war with Mexico in 1846 and in the war with North Korea in 1950. It is certainly arguable, with regard to the first of these struggles, that had not President Polk sent General Taylor into the no-man's land between the Nueces and the Rio Grande a clash might have been avoided. In the second case, a less resolute and definite-minded President than Harry Truman might have hesitated to take up the challenge to the United Nations presented by the invasion of South Korea. It is possible, of course, to question the wisdom of each of these decisions.

All in all, however, the great power of the President has not been exercised, so far as the weightiest of all decisions, the decision to make war, is concerned, in such a fashion as to call for highly critical comment or to suggest that no account was taken of American public opinion. But has a President, in the exercise of his prerogative, taken decisions that have damaged the prestige of the United States or violated the principles of democratic government? It is hard to believe so. President McKinley committed the nation to a certain extent to an imperialist course in the peace protocol of 1898. But the question of the Philippines, we have seen, was kept open, and in the Senate and in the election of 1900 public sentiment seems to have been with the chief executive. President Roosevelt defied the Senate on the Dominican question in 1905, but the Senate of 1907 ratified a treaty which was virtually in accord with his policy. The

Fourteen Points and the armistice negotiations in accordance with them were certainly in line with public opinion. One cannot, in a brief essay, review the whole course of American foreign policy to discuss this question in great detail. But there is, I think, in recent years only one instance where the action of the executive ran counter, in all probability, to the views of a very large number of Americans. When, at Yalta, President Roosevelt agreed to the assumption by Russia of important rights in the Chinese province of Manchuria, he may have had valid reasons, in his own conscience, for doing so, since such a concession seemed necessary to bring the Soviet Union into the war against Japan. But the secrecy which surrounded this whole transaction, which was carried so far that a copy of the agreement was never even filed with the State Department, suggests that behind this diplomatic deal was an uneasy feeling that the whole business would be reprobated by a large body of Americans. This kind of personal negotiation, in fact, goes very far indeed; I venture to think that few Presidents would have the self-assurance to make such sweeping commitments, and I do not know of any other President who has done so. The American people, I am sure, would strongly denounce this kind of personal diplomacy and the bargaining away of the rights or interests of a third party, if they were kept informed.

Our analysis of the vast powers of the President, pointed up by the negotiations at Yalta, raises the question of whether the President ought to be an expert in diplomatic matters and whether this should be taken into account in the selection of the chief executive. Before we answer this question, we might well look at the record and see what it shows. General Washington had had no direct diplomatic experience, in the literal sense. The five Presidents who followed him, on the contrary, had had much. John Adams had conducted important negotiations throughout the Revolution and had put his name to the treaty of peace. Jefferson had been Minister to France and Secretary of State before he became President. Madison had been Secretary of State under Jefferson, and Monroe Secretary of State under Madison, as well as Minister to France in the 1790's and Minister to both Spain and Britain under Jefferson. John Quincy Adams had had the widest experience of all, Minister to Prussia, the Netherlands, Russia, and Great Britain, and Secretary of State to boot. But from Adams on, few of the chief executives had much diplomatic training. Van Buren had been Minister to Great Britain, and Buchanan both a foreign representative of the United States and Secretary of State under Polk. But Jackson, Harrison, Tyler, Polk, Taylor, Fillmore, and Pierce had never had any responsibility for the conduct of foreign policy or served the country abroad before they became President. From Lincoln's day to the present not a single President has had any very large experience in affairs diplomatic. Taft had been on a quasi-diplomatic mission to the Vatican and as Secretary of War had carried on negotiations with Japan. Hoover had participated in international negotiations, in the broad sense, in connection with his Belgian relief mission, and played a subordinate part—hardly that of a negotiator—in the peace conference of Paris in 1919. Does the record show that, in general, the conduct of our foreign relations was carried on with most success by the Presidents who possessed the greatest experience in this field? I do not think so. Madison was most inept in the Presidency from this point of view. John Quincy Adams, a great Secretary of State, accomplished little as chief executive. There is not much to be said for Buchanan. On the other hand, Andrew

Jackson's administrations, under a chief executive whose previous career might well have suggested serious limitations, were notable for their dignified and, on the whole, restrained diplomacy. Taken altogether, Lincoln's tenure of office was marked by really excellent handling of the country's interests, and so on the whole was Grant's. And the three Presidents who left the deepest mark, Wilson and the two Roosevelts, were completely without diplomatic training. As one looks at the total record, then, there seems no reason to maintain that previous participation in international negotiation is an indispensable quality in the leader of the nation. At any rate, since the early days of the republic, the practice has run contrary to any such assumption.

Is there any way in which we can make sure in advance of the capacity and wisdom which the great Presidents have displayed in the field of foreign affairs? Certainly, the machinery by which the American people select a President is not specially adapted to such a purpose. Political expediency is the dominating force in national nominating conventions and, where personal ability is considered, it is rarely the type of ability that guarantees success in dealing with the affairs of diplomacy. Even in these days, when questions of foreign policy are more important than they have ever before been, the competence of a candidate in this field is not likely to weigh heavily with the great majority of the delegates.

In one respect, however, we may be better off than we were in the nineteenth century, or even forty years ago. Foreign affairs, in the last four decades, have come to play an increasingly important part in the Presidential campaigns and in the public mind. We may, therefore, find in the previous record of an aspirant for the Presidency more than a few hints as to whether he is provincial and parochial or large in his understanding of such matters. We may be better able than we once were to estimate his abilities by the character of his public speeches in the campaign itself. We may find in the platform of his party some measure of guidance as to what course he will pursue. It is certainly desirable that these things be considered by the intelligent voter; for on decisions in matters of foreign policy the health of the nation may well depend. But it is not likely that we shall always be able to judge wisely, even if we care about these things. Political campaigns are rarely distinguished by the clarification of public issues; on the contrary, the purpose of the candidates is often to confuse rather than instruct, to equivocate rather than speak out boldly. Senator Harding in 1920 managed to persuade both pro-League and anti-League Republicans that they should vote for him. An analysis of the speeches of Wendell Willkie and Franklin Roosevelt in the campaign of 1940 does not raise one's opinion of the sincerity of either candidate, though, in Roosevelt's case, the citizen had at least the benefit of a record by which to be guided. The duty of the citizen is at all times difficult to discharge, if performed with a true sense of public responsibility; and it would be romantic to imagine that the voters will always choose well, so far as matters of foreign policy are concerned. Indeed, a large part of the electorate, the great bulk of it, we may say, will probably be much more influenced by other issues than by any question of diplomacy, unless perhaps it is the great issue of war and peace.

Nonetheless, we do not need to give way to pessimism. In the critical periods of its history, the nation has done well; and even if we are not always so fortunate as we have been, even a small man in the Presidency feels the challenge of his responsibility and is likely to grow in stature and in wisdom under the pressure of great events.

To a degree, moreover, limitations in the capacity of the chief executive may be made up for by the choice of a highly competent Secretary of State. They may never be *wholly* made up for, since no Secretary, however wise or able, can address the people of the United States with the same authority as the President, or carry quite the same weight with the leaders of the party in Congress or with the opposition. But there have been several occasions in American history when Presidents of limited experience in foreign affairs have given wide authority to their appointees, and when the policy of the nation has been wisely conducted as a result. This was true, for example, in the period of Lincoln's Presidency. Most of the decisions were Seward's, especially after the first few months, the executive interposing on relatively rare occasions. Grant, altogether inept in diplomacy, was saved from many errors by his Secretary, Hamilton Fish; Harding, one of the most ignorant of the occupants of the White House, gave to Charles Evans Hughes a very wide authority, with the result that foreign affairs were conducted with the highest competence. Eisenhower's weaknesses in the diplomatic field were partially atoned for by the substantial abilities of John Foster Dulles. Certainly, in quiet times, the deficiencies of the executive can be made up for in some degree by his wise choice of a subordinate.

On the other hand, the strongest Presidents have perhaps frequently leaned less than they ought to upon the State Department. In the administration of Woodrow Wilson, Lansing, and perhaps in some respects Bryan before him, was hardly more than a chief clerk, and much of the most important business was transacted through the President's personal adviser, Colonel House. President Franklin D. Roosevelt took much authority to himself, gave to his confidant, Harry Hopkins, a wide scope of activity, and sometimes bypassed Secretary Hull in ways that could hardly fail to be galling. It is, I think, a question whether this kind of personal diplomacy is always wise. There is a place for the professional in the conduct of diplomacy, and to thrust him too much to one side is to deprive oneself of much useful information, and often of highly suggestive and valuable points of view. The President has a right to lead, if he can; but he will lead more wisely if he leans upon his advisers, at least in the sense that he gets their assessment of a given situation before he acts and weighs it seriously in his own mind.

But what of the Secretary of State himself? What kind of man may best serve as the first lieutenant of the executive in the field of foreign relations? Is it a technician that we want in this post, to supplement the more generalized view of his chief? Again, a survey of the past does not suggest an affirmative answer. The author has sought from some of the leading scholars of the field an evaluation of the various holders of the office. The persons most frequently commended were John Quincy Adams, Hamilton Fish, Thomas Jefferson, Elihu Root, Charles Evans Hughes, William H. Seward, John Hay, and Daniel Webster. Of these eight, only three had had diplomatic experience. One was J. Q. Adams, by common account the greatest Secretary of State. But Seward, Fish, and Hughes, all of them men of accepted competence, had never been particularly concerned with questions of foreign affairs when they entered the State Department. The truth of the matter is that it is more important for the Secretary to have qualities of insight and wisdom than technical knowledge. He must (and this is a matter of native intelligence rather than special training) know how to weigh the materials which come to him, judge shrewdly what is practicable and what is not; he must have the capacity for stating the issues persuasively and be able to meet foreign diplomats with courteous understanding, while maintaining the point of view most consistent with the national interest; he must also (and this is important) know how to get along with Congress; in other words, he must possess the political gifts. In their way Philander Knox and Frank B. Kellogg were men of ability. But too often they rasped the susceptibilities of the leaders at the other end of Pennsylvania Avenue, and their by no means brilliant discharge of their responsibilities was due in no small measure to this fact. The better record of Cordell Hull (who can hardly be ranked as a great figure intellectually) sprang in no small degree from his familiarity with the ways of politicians and from the sympathetic understanding that he could often command at the Capitol. The highest qualities of statesmanship are connected with some kind of subtle comprehension of the public mind and of individual minds; they are, in a way, elusive; and it is therefore no more possible to prescribe exactly what makes a great Secretary than it is to determine who will make a great President. All that can be said is that in choosing his chief adviser in the field of foreign policy, the executive may, on occasion, wisely give more weight to political than to diplomatic experience, to sound judgment and true insight rather than to specialized knowledge.

This is not to argue, of course, that the Secretary should be a mere party hack or that every party leader is fitted for the post. The appointment of Robert Smith by Madison was scandalous, altogether a result of factional rather than more significant considerations. When President McKinley kicked the venerable John Sherman upstairs from the Senate to the State Department to make way for Mark Hanna under the dome of the Capitol, he did little to advance the foreign interests of the United States. There will be some who doubt whether Wilson's choice of Bryan in 1913 was an entirely happy one, eminent as the Great Commoner had been in Democratic politics and beholden to him as the President was. The office ought not to be treated, as it has at times been treated, as a reward for party service. But neither should it be completely divorced from politics. It is the blend of politics and statesmanship that is needed, however difficult it may be to find.

We must consider, at least for a moment, the role of State Department personnel in the formulation of policy. The subject, like the organization of the department, is a complicated one. When one looks at the matter over the hundred and seventy-odd years of this country's existence, it is reasonably clear that for a very long period the part played by the Secretary's subordinates was not very great. Men like Hunter and Adee may have played a greater role than we can discern, but I know of no evidence that they actually shaped decisively any major decisions. But the situation had begun to change in the twentieth century. It is not possible to state with certainty where the Roosevelt corollary with regard to the Monroe Doctrine actually originated. But there are clear signs that an assistant secretary of state had something to do with it and that the influence of subordinate officials in the department was exerted in its behalf in the Taft and Wilson administrations. It is also reasonably clear that, in the formulation of our policy towards Germany in 1914 and early 1915, the President preferred the advice of Lansing, then counsellor in the department and a specialist in international law, to the advice of the less experienced Bryan. It is also obvious that in the movement towards the reversal of the Roosevelt corollary, which began in the days of the Hughes secretariat, Sumner Welles played a very important role and that he left his mark upon department personnel even after he had resigned in 1922. The influence of Welles, indeed, was even greater at a later period in the formulation of the good-neighbor policy and, when he resigned for the second time in 1943, our policy in Latin America, especially in relation to Argentina, swerved away from the principles which he had espoused. In the drafting of the Charter of the United Nations, the scant attention paid to the republics of the New World and the resulting resentments were due in no small degree to one of the officials of the department who was charged with the preparatory work on this important project. In the drafting of the Marshall Plan George Kennan, the chairman of the Policy Committee (a newly formed division of the department), played a substantial and significant role.

The influence of the subordinate members of the department may be described in another way. Every decision is both an act of will and an act of intelligence. In regard to the second, what matters—and matters tremendously—is where the official responsible for action gets his information and how good that information is. In this sense a heavy responsibility rests upon the department personnel and upon our diplomatic representatives abroad. There was a time when this personnel was recruited in a haphazard fashion and when diplomatic posts were treated as political patronage. Today, for the most part, the diplomatic service is professional. Ambassadorships are sometimes awarded to generous campaign contributors, and for the great posts it is still not uncommon to select a political supporter whose large means enable him to maintain an establishment and a style of living for which Congress fails to provide. Yet, with rare exceptions, it seems fair to say that the quality and competence of State Department personnel is creditable and worthy of commendation.

But today it is quite impossible to conduct the foreign policy of the United States through the activities of the State Department alone. For example, questions of defense play a large part in the determination of foreign policy. A political decision cannot be dissociated from a military posture. It is natural, therefore—indeed, indispensable—that the Department of Defense be consulted. To take another example, many of the most difficult questions of foreign policy deal with economic matters. Such questions may involve such agencies as the Export-Import Bank, which dispenses loans to foreign countries, or the United States Tariff Commission, which has important powers with regard to the duties to be laid upon imports. The list of agencies which, in one way or another, impinge upon foreign policy could, indeed, be indefinitely extended. And this is to say nothing of the fact that, in addition to the role of other executive agencies, the President and the Secretary must find a way of dealing with a congress which is naturally jealous of its powers and which controls the budget, and with a public opinion which demands to be consulted and whose support is indispensable to the effective implementation of policy.

We shall deal with some of these matters in another chapter. But mention is necessary here of two governmental bodies which have developed great significance in the period since the war and which alter substantially the policy-making process.

One of these is the Central Intelligence Agency, which, growing out of the Office of Strategic Services constituted during the war, has become in all probability an even more important fact-gathering agency than the State Department, employing fully as many employees and provided with a substantially larger budget. Part of the work of the CIA is espionage, which is, of course, practiced by every government and which involves the use of methods that are not always nice. But a far greater part of the activity of the agency consists in amassing vast amounts of information from public sources, from governmental reports, from other governmental agencies, including the State Department and other agencies abroad, and from military sources. The evaluation of this great mass of material constitutes an immense task, and on the Director of Central Intelligence there rests a very heavy burden. Miscalculations there are bound to be, and not only miscalculations but failure to give due emphasis to this or that piece of information received. But the collecting and interpretation of the data is an indispensable part of the foreign-policy process.

A question recently raised is as to whether the CIA should combine the collecting and evaluation of intelligence with operative functions. This it appeared to have done in the Cuban imbroglio of 1960–61. The Cuban exiles who aimed at the overthrow of the government of Fidel Castro were given arms and instruction by representatives of the agency, and were indeed encouraged in the making of plans for an invasion. The invasion, when it came, was a terrible fiasco. The strength of the Castro regime had been egregiously underestimated; the extent of public discontent in Cuba had been enormously exaggerated. The CIA had become the victim of its own prepossessions and desires. In this instance, it had had a major role in determining policy, and the State Department, so it would appear, had acquiesced in its recommendations. Criticism of the technique employed was widespread.

Another agency which impinges in a most important way on policy is the National Security Council, created by an act of Congress in 1947. Recognizing the interrelation of foreign policy and national defense, the act created a council of which the statutory members are the President and Vice-President, the Secretaries of State and Defense, and the Director of the Office of Civil and Defense Mobilization. The Chairman of the Joint Chiefs of Staff, (in other words, the highest military official of the government) and the Director of Central Intelligence are statutory advisers to the council. Other persons may be invited to attend, and under President Eisenhower the Secretary of the Treasury, the Director of the Budget, and the Chairman of the Atomic Energy Commission were normally participants in the deliberations of the council. There exists also a large staff, under an Executive Secretary, which prepares position papers on important questions of policy.

The National Security Council does not *decide;* decision must rest, in the last analysis, with the President, the Secretary of State or of Defense, or with some other executive officer of the government. The nature of the conclusions arrived at in the Council will vary with the force of personality of the individuals concerned, with the depth of their knowledge, and, of course, with the temperament of the President himself. Both Truman and Eisenhower have paid tribute to the importance of the new instrument of policy; each has used it in his own way.

This institution is too new to warrant large generalizations as to its actual operation. On the one hand, it seems to be a necessary instrumentality for coordinating the various agencies which have, inevitably, a vital role in the formulation of policy; on the other hand, it may tend to make actual decision more difficult, amidst a diversity of views. The injection of financial officers into its debates may be justified as the recognition of a substantial reality; on the other hand, it may give to fiscal considerations an undue influence in the formation of policy. No institution is stronger than the individuals composing it; the role of personal ability, and personal force, must always be of the highest importance.

In essence, indeed, the great decisions in foreign policy will, in the nature of the case, be made by a few men. Behind these men will be other men, who, by providing them with the data on which they base their action, play a highly important role. Many of the answers to the central questions must be found *in camera*, and sometimes without time for deliberation and under a crushing burden of doubt as to whether one has all the facts. Once again, then, there is no substitute for personal ability, courage, dedication, soundness of judgment, and mastery of the data.

Does this vitiate the assumption which we made in an earlier chapter that foreign policy in the United States to an extraordinary degree comes up from the people? I do not think so. The most powerful official operates, and the most portentous decisions are taken, within a frame of reference and a climate of opinion which is of transcendent importance. There was, for example, much official opinion in the State Department until the Korean episode in favor of a policy of recognition of the Chinese Communists. But it was not possible to carry through any such policy in practice. Public prejudices were too strong. There was an attempt at a modus vivendi with Japan just before Pearl Harbor. But it would not have been possible for the administration to face the American public if it had acquiesced in such an arrangement. No diplomatic officer today could with safety propose a program of "appeasement" with Russia. And, in addition to all this, while decisions can be taken and the government committed, there is always Congress, the sounding board of public opinion and the jealous guardian of popular government, in the offing. Sooner or later, in the course of events, it is to this body that the officials must turn for support and for sustained prosecution of the policy which they initiate. We shall have to turn, then, from an examination of the role of the executive in foreign affairs to an examination of the place of the national legislature, and of the masses from which that legislature derives its authority and whose moods and aspirations and interests it naturally seeks to serve.

IX

The Legislature and Public Opinion
in American Foreign Policy

————————◆·◄◆►·◆————————

A s we have seen in the preceding chapter, the President of the United States is a powerful figure in the field of foreign relations. By his power to conduct negotiations he can shape the course of policy; through the use of personal agents, through the use of executive agreements, and through the use of his war powers, he possesses an immense authority. But the President acts, as we have seen, within the framework of public opinion and of the democratic political habits which are deeply ingrained in the American mind; and he is subject, too, to certain other restraints. One of these is the duty to submit treaties to the Senate for its advice and consent; a second is the necessity of securing, sooner or later, in the nature of the case, the necessary funds for the carrying on of his policies and the legislative approval which is often equally imperative. We cannot, then, understand the American system in relation to foreign affairs without studying the place of the national legislature in relation to American diplomacy, and we may well begin by examining the special role of the Senate.

The Senate exercises, under the Constitution, two powers with regard to treaties which ought to be considered separately from one another. Ever since 1794, it has asserted the right to amend the international compacts that are submitted to it, in advance of advising and consenting to them by a vote of two thirds of its members. Both the amending power and the two-thirds rule have come under considerable criticism. It is worth while to examine each.

Let us look first at the power of amendment. Numerically speaking, the Senate has not altered most treaties submitted to it. As Royden Dangerfield points out in his interesting book, *In Defense of the Senate*, the number amounts to only about 16 percent of the whole. Nor is the process of amendment always a disservice to the interests of the United States. In the case of the Jay Treaty, for example, the Senate struck out a provision which would have seriously restricted the commerce of the United States without providing any countervailing advantages—for John Jay, in order to open the West Indian trade to the Americans (and this only to very small vessels), had agreed that the United States would not export a number of raw materials, among which was cotton. A still more striking case in which the Senate acted wisely was in amending the first Hay-Pauncefote Treaty relative to the construction of an interoceanic canal. It disapproved particularly of the provision of this treaty which forbade the fortification of the canal. John Hay, it is true, was much upset at this, and it is in connection with this episode that he made his famous and oft-quoted remark that a "third of the Senate was always to be found on the blackguard side of any question." But John Hay, always prone to harsh and melancholy judgment, was, of course, wrong. For as a result of the defeat of the first treaty, he was compelled to negotiate a second one, and this compact gave by silence the right to construct fortifications in the canal zone. Who can doubt that this was to the advantage of the United States?

There is, it is true, a certain type of treaty which long had rough sledding in the upper house. Arbitration treaties and kindred compacts, such as the World Court protocol, usually were badly damaged by the process of amendment in the Senate. President McKinley, for instance, submitted in 1897 a new and improved type of arbitration treaty with Great Britain. It was denatured almost beyond recognition. President Roosevelt, in 1904, submitted a series of treaties, and the Senate took the heart out of them by providing that, in each individual case of arbitration which might take place under them, the protocol of arbitration must itself be submitted for advice and consent. President Taft in 1910–11 negotiated a series of compacts, which were an advance on previous agreements in that they submitted the question of what was arbitrable to an international body for decision and which, in the case of the British accord, had the additional advantage of curtailing the effect of the British-Japanese treaty of alliance and making it inapplicable against the United States. But the mutilations and qualifications introduced and passed by way of amendment ended all hope of usefulness for the whole series.

The record of the period after World War I was, in some respects, still less savory. It would be too long a matter to analyze in detail the reservations, as they were called, appended to the Treaty of Versailles. It must always be a disputed question whether these reservations could have been accepted by the powers concerned, if the treaty had been ratified. But the spirit which presided over the debates on these reservations was often narrowly nationalistic, and inconceivably petty, and there can be little doubt that it was the intention of at least some senators on the Republican side to make the treaty unacceptable to President Wilson, an intention of course that was realized. The antics of the Senate on the World Court protocol were still more open to criticism. The World Court had been set up for some years and was actually functioning, with the active support of most of the nations of the world, when the upper house first voted on a resolution of adherence in 1926. Yet the proposal of the administration was so altered as to be unacceptable to the other powers, and when, after years of negotiation, the difficulties between the United States and the nations supporting the court were resolved and a new agreement submitted to the Senate, this agreement was defeated. On this issue, it seems to me, there can be little defense for the upper house.

Let us turn to a consideration of the two-thirds rule. We may well begin with a word or two as to its origins. Why was it incorporated into the Constitution of the United States by the framers? In one sense, it was merely a continuation of a principle already stated in the Articles of Confederation, by which the assent of nine states was required for all important decisions. In the second place, representation in the Senate being on the basis of equality, it was argued in the Constitutional Convention that a minority of the people of the United States might bind a majority to an international agreement which was widely opposed. The argument had, of course, no more force with regard to treaties than with regard to acts of ordinary legislation. But it was reinforced by a powerful sentiment. Fundamentally, the men of 1787 were isolationist in their point of view, the representatives of a political system that had hardly been tried elsewhere and of a continent still remote from the affairs of the Old World. They had, many of them, a congenital distrust of Europe. They wished the diplomatic activities of the United States to be kept to a minimum. Men as different in temperament as Jefferson and Gouverneur Morris (Jefferson, it should be said parenthetically, was not at the convention) were to be found expressing the same view. The general assumption that treaties would not be and ought not to be numerous had something, perhaps much, to do with the provisions of the Constitution.

The two-thirds rule of the Senate caused very little debate in the course of the nineteenth century. But it came under hot discussion after the defeat of the Treaty of Versailles and stimulated a debate of very wide proportions. It was claimed that a Senate majority could first mutilate a treaty by amendment, so that when it came before the Senate for ratification a two-thirds vote could not possibly be secured. But the argument does not seem to be very conclusive. For, speaking generally, it would appear that if there were a majority in favor of changes in a given compact, this same majority would be able to prevent ratification if compelled to vote upon it without emendation. The true test of the undesirability of the two-thirds rule, so it appears to me, is to be found by analyzing those cases in which a treaty was rejected which had behind it a majority, but not the requisite constitutional majority of the Senate.

If we apply this criterion the two-thirds rule does not appear to be of any considerable significance. In the one hundred and seventy-three years of our national history, only four treaties have been defeated where a majority of the Senate voted for ratification. One was a treaty of compulsory arbitration with Great Britain, submitted by President McKinley and defeated by 43 affirmative and 26 negative votes. A second was a claims convention with Mexico, in which the poll was 32 to 26. A third was the protocol providing for American adherence to the World Court, on which the vote was 52 to 36. The fourth, and of course the most striking, was the vote on the Treaty of Versailles, which was approved with reservations by the Senate in March by the inadequate vote of 49 to 36. In this last instance, it is easy to feel considerable indignation, if one inclines to the view that the history of the postwar years after 1919 might have been happier if the United States had entered the League of Nations. But a more cautious judgment is necessary for the historian. For it is by no means clear beyond all peradventure of a doubt that the treaty with reservations would have been acceptable to other governments, and it is therefore not clear that the failure of the resolution of ratification was an unmitigated disaster. And to assume that the vote would have been the same had the two-thirds rule not existed is also a somewhat dubious conclusion. All in all, then, even this instance in which the rule prevented action is not so impressive as is sometimes supposed.

It is sometimes said that treaties are not submitted to the Senate or not reported out of committee because of the difficulties inherent in the two-thirds requirement. But Professor Dangerfield, who has considered this argument, rightly declares that it would be very difficult to prove this thesis. Nor do I know of any cases where this could be demonstrated.

But, perhaps, in any case, we ought not to take the question too seriously. For there are, and indeed have been, for some time ways of avoiding the difficulty of the two-thirds rule when it seems desirable to do so. One of these is the executive agreement, discussed in a preceding chapter. But there is another expedient, less arbitrary in its nature, which is taking root in our practice and which bids fair to play a more and more significant part as time goes on. It was first employed in 1844. In that year, John C. Calhoun, then Secretary of State, submitted the Texas treaty to the Senate. As we have seen, the treaty was defeated. But after the election of 1844, the American people having voted for that party which had outspokenly endorsed the annexation of Texas, the Congress of the United States admitted Texas to the Union by joint resolution, this resolution, of course, requiring no more than a mere majority of both houses of Congress. The example of the Texas resolution was not followed, at any rate on an important issue, for a long time after 1845. But in 1898, in the ebullient nationalism of the period of the Spanish-American War, it was desired to annex Hawaii. Again the votes for a treaty were not to be found in the Senate. Accordingly, Congress again passed a joint resolution, going one step further than it had in 1845, from the standpoint of constitutional procedure. For the right of the national legislature to admit new *states* was written into the Constitution. But the organization of a territory outside the bounds of the United States was another matter, and yet this was precisely what was done. Thus the senatorial opposition was outflanked.

There have been many, many examples of this procedure in the last forty years. One of the earliest cases, after the First World War, was the enactment of the agreements refunding the debts owed by its various European allies to the United States, by acts of ordinary legislation. Still more important and more dramatic was the passage of the famous lend-lease measure in the spring of 1941. In this case we virtually entered into a quasi-alliance with Great Britain by statute, instead of by treaty. Again, in the period after the Second World War, such important measures as the providing of aid to Greece and Turkey and the appropriations for the Marshall Plan were passed by both houses of Congress, though they certainly touch very nearly the treaty-making power. The furnishing of arms aid to Europe, upon which the country embarked in 1949, has been carried on by the purely legislative process.

What is still more interesting is that Congress, in recent years, has given to the President the power to make agreements which do not require senatorial action. For example, by the various reciprocal-trade-agreement acts, beginning in 1934, the President is empowered to enter into negotiations with other states for the reciprocal lowering of tariff duties, and these negotiations may result in accords which automatically become binding. In the case of the Lend-Lease Act, the chief executive was enabled to make special arrangements with individual countries within the general terms of the law. In other words, not only has lawmaking taken the place of treatymaking, but lawmaking has authorized a kind of treatymaking which is still more curious, and this kind of thing has awakened a very minimum of protest, even on the part of senators themselves. Have we here a recognition of the fact that we need a more expeditious and certain method of dealing with international questions? Perhaps so. Yet we must not think that treatymaking is by any means becoming obsolete. The Charter of the United Nations was duly submitted to the Senate. The satellite treaties with Bulgaria, Rumania, Hungary, and Italy, all ran the gauntlet of senatorial action. And, most important of all, the Atlantic Defense Treaty was presented to the upper house for its approval. If one turns to matters of less pith and moment, moreover, one would find that there are still scores of agreements that run the ordinary course. We have done no more than develop an alternative method, and a very convenient method at that, for dealing with some of the more important problems of foreign policy.

The new technique which we have just been examining might be thought to strengthen the hand of the President and make easier his conduct of the foreign policy of the nation. Perhaps it does, but this is not always the case. For the power of Congress to legislate is not always exercised at the suggestion of the executive; it may be exercised independently of the executive. Congress, indeed, has at certain times exerted a strong influence on foreign policy, and it is entirely conceivable that it might do so again. The balance between the authority of the White House and the authority of the Capitol, though more frequently tipped in favor of the former today than in early times, is never a certain one and can be perceptibly altered even under a strong leader. The lawmaking power may in certain cases be more determinative of policy than the action of the President himself.

Perhaps the most interesting example of this in relatively recent times is to be found in the neutrality legislation of the middle thirties. It is well known that President Roosevelt and Secretary Hull ardently desired that, if prohibitions were to be placed on the export of arms or war materials, discretionary power be placed in the hands of the executive to apply such bans against an aggressor, rather than against aggressor and aggressed alike. Yet Congress decided otherwise. In this respect, and indeed in some others, it enacted statutes which were most certainly distasteful to the White House and, by so doing, gave assurance to Hitler and to Mussolini that they might pursue their course of aggrandizement without any interference on the part of the United States. True, this legislation was modified after the outbreak of war in 1939; but it stands as an extraordinary example, nonetheless, of the way in which the policy of the government may be fixed at the other end of Pennsylvania Avenue from the White House.

There are, I think, few cases in which Congress has gone so far to define foreign policy, in action independent of the executive, as that of the enactments I have just mentioned. But it was certainly Congress, and not the executive, which was determining policy in matters of the same sort in the Presidency of James Madison, though there was no definite conflict of view. And there have been other occasions, as in the case of the Chinese Exclusion Act of 1882, when the leaders at the Capitol attempted to seize the initiative and to enact measures which were by no means congenial to the executive.

It must always be remembered, moreover, that Congress possesses the appropriating power. To grant or withhold "supply," as the British put it, is obviously a very large matter indeed. Broadly speaking, most Presidents have not had a very difficult time from this point of view so far as foreign affairs are concerned. But the matter may be important. In the last few years, for example, the debates on foreign aid have often been quite sharp, and the administration has been by no means certain to get all that it asks. The action of the two houses on measures of defense may or may not be entirely congenial to the administration. The sums granted may be less or more than demanded, and they may be differently distributed from the way the administration desires. The decisions taken on such matters may, of course, have sharp repercussions abroad and may, and sometimes do, offer a very real hindrance to effective action on the part of the State Department or the White House. The guiding hand in our diplomacy usually comes from the executive; but no executive, not even the strongest, can possibly fail to consult the opinion of the legislative body, and even the strongest may at times be hampered by it.

The question of the proper relationship between the legislative and the executive in matters of foreign policy is one that has by no means been worked out to perfection under our constitutional system. The procedure under which we operate is an extremely cumbrous one. One might cite the machinery employed in connection with foreign aid. There has had to be passed in both Houses, first of all, an authorization bill. But this authorization bill is no more than a declaration of intention on the part of Congress. It does not make a single penny available to the executive, and must be followed by an appropriation bill. Each of these measures must be preceded by hearings in both houses. In extreme cases, the Secretary himself may be called upon to testify four separate times on a measure which he deems to be of vital interest. Even if less important officials are involved, the whole business is an extremely time-consuming one. It tends, too, to put the Secretary, or those who speak for him, at a very substantial disadvantage. The senators or congressmen who are most active in the work of interrogation are often those who have least sympathy with the purposes of the administration. Their questions are often framed to embarrass or irritate, rather than with an eye to an objective appraisal of the subject in hand. If the officer under questioning makes a slip, it is sure to be exploited. If he shows resentment, even justifiable resentment, at the ignorance or the bad spirit of one of the national legislators, he is likely to have to pay for it. Even if he be fatigued, and under severe strain, he must school himself to a serenity which is not always easy to practice.

It has sometimes been suggested that it would be desirable for the Secretary to appear directly before one or the other of the two houses to explain his policies. Indeed, on one occasion, Secretary Acheson did meet with the members of both House and Senate, so far as they chose to appear, in one of the halls of the Library of Congress. He first outlined the international situation and then submitted to interrogation. But the experiment was only moderately successful. The Secretary was not wholly at ease; and the questions asked added very little to the sum total of human knowledge and, in some instances, seemed to show that the honorable gentlemen before him had not been listening very carefully to what he had to say.

A better expedient is that which has been more practiced, that the members of the two committees on foreign affairs be continuously briefed on the course of events, and that the committees be subdivided into groups which concern themselves with certain specific areas or problems in the field of policy. The difficulty here lies in the propensity of congressmen to discuss in public what they are told in secret, but this whole problem of secrecy is one which we must discuss in more detail a little later.

In determining the relations of the executive with the legislature, and the effectiveness of congressional cooperation, one factor of great importance is the composition and leadership of the appropriate committees in House and Senate, especially in the latter body. The chairman of the Senate Committee on Foreign Relations wields a very substantial power. Charles Sumner, for example, in this office, was a thorn in the flesh of the Grant administration and gravely embarrassed its conduct of affairs, especially the negotiations with Great Britain over the *Alabama* claims. So serious, indeed, was his opposition that he was eventually demoted. Profound as was the party hostility to

President Wilson in 1919, the presence of Senator Lodge as chairman of the Senate committee added to the embitterment of the atmosphere in the debate on the Treaty of Versailles. Senator Borah was perhaps more influential than the Secretary of State himself in the second Coolidge administration. The early days of the Franklin Roosevelt administration were made no easier by the fact that Senator Pittman of Nevada occupied the key post in the Senate. On the other hand, the granting of aid to Greece and Turkey and the development of the Marshall Plan owed much to the political skill and firm convictions of Senator Vandenberg. Though of a different party from the administration, he gave his high abilities to the development of a truly national policy towards Europe and carried many other Republicans in the Senate with him. One could, of course, exaggerate the importance of these personal factors. Senators are, after all, American politicians, and where public opinion is clearly expressed, they are apt to bow to it. But there is, as we have seen, always an area of action in the field of foreign affairs where no clear public judgment has been expressed, and within this area the views of individuals are bound to be important.

The chairmen of the committees in House and Senate which deal with foreign affairs are, of course, chosen chiefly on the basis of seniority. It is certainly not one of the strongest points of our political system that this is so. No doubt, something is to be gained through length of service, but length of service is not, unfortunately, any guarantee of special competence. Still more, it by no means guarantees agreement with the views of the administration. Even when the administration and the Senate majority are of the same political faith, there is, as we have already said, plenty of possibility for discord. And if they are of different partisan loyalties, the danger of disagreement is still greater.

This whole question of partisanship in diplomatic matters is worth our thoughtful consideration. The record of partisan antagonism to the course of the administration goes back a very long way, indeed. The wars of the French Revolution deeply divided American public opinion, and the policy of General Washington, which moved towards an understanding with Great Britain, was sharply and bitterly criticized. In the same way, when Federalist policy under John Adams moved towards a breach with France, almost every vote in Congress found the members of the majority party aligned solidly on one side and the Democratic Republicans on the other. The party habit was still more revealingly displayed when the Federalists opposed the 1803 treaty of cession, although they had been ready to denounce the administration of Thomas Jefferson for weakness in not acting more vigorously against the Spanish government in Louisiana, when it suspended the American right of free deposit in New Orleans of goods for transshipment. The policy of the embargo also was from the beginning a matter of partisan rivalry. And, as we have already seen, Federalist opposition to the War of 1812 went so far as to hamper seriously the conduct of hostilities and to put some strain upon the fabric of the Union itself.

The "era of good feeling," naturally, was marked by a cessation of sharp rivalry in foreign as in domestic affairs. But, when John Quincy Adams came into power, the battle of the factions was renewed. The proposal of the President to send delegates to the Pan-American Congress at Panama in 1826 became the subject of a furious debate, in which political maneuvering played a more important part than any question of principle. Nor were the Whigs slow to take advantage of an opening in the days of Andrew Jackson. A quarrel with France over the payment of the spoliation claims was handled, on the whole, with considerable skill, and with no great risk on the part of the administration. But Henry Clay and his followers raised a great hue and cry over the possibility of war and sought to make capital at home out of a matter of diplomacy. Texas, too, became a party issue, and so did the Mexican War.

The partisan spirit in matters of foreign policy persisted up to very recent times. It was exemplified in the debates on the peace treaty with Spain; it played a part in the evolution of our Caribbean policy; it was present in the period of the First World War; and, of course, it was rampant in the debates over the Treaty of Versailles. In the twenties, the Democrats were more moderate in their attitude towards the Republican foreign policy of the period than had generally been the case, historically speaking, with their rivals, and there were signs of bipartisan cooperation on such matters as the disarmament negotiations of 1922 and 1930, as well as with regard to the war-debt question. But, in the years just preceding the entry of the United States into the Second World War, there was a good deal of political maneuvering. In the vote on the arms embargo in 1939, in the vote on the conscription bill in 1941, in the vote on Lend-Lease in 1941, and in the vote on the arming of merchant ships and the abolition of the zones from which American shipping was excluded, in the late fall of 1941, many more Republicans voted in opposition than Democrats, and this was particularly true in the House of Representatives.

In the last twenty years the feeling that factious criticism is undesirable, and that there is a case for bipartisanship in matters of diplomacy, has tended to take root. Our Latin

American policy has now been for some time, with very limited exceptions, a matter of united action. The policy of the good neighbor, the beginnings of which were clearly adumbrated in the days of Charles Evans Hughes's secretariat, and in the Morrow mission and the Clark memorandum, has rested for the most part on the basis of general approval. The protocols of Montevideo and Buenos Aires, for example, were ratified by the unanimous vote of the Senate, and there was scarcely any opposition to the later understandings at Chapultepec and at Rio.

In European matters, moreover, the coming of the war saw a very considerable relaxation of partisan rivalry, even though this relaxation did not extend to the hard-bitten Republican leadership in the House of Representatives. In the campaign of 1940, the nomination of Wendell Willkie made it clear that the issue of American aid to Europe would not become a matter of political debate, and the despatch of Willkie to Europe by the President in 1941 gave a nonpolitical flavor, to some degree, to the discussion of Lend-Lease, despite (once more be it said) the obscurantism of the Martins and Hallecks in the lower house. In the campaign of 1944 Governor Dewey, to his credit, indulged in no cheap attempt at capitalizing on foreign issues, though there was occasional sniping. The drafting of the Charter of the United Nations was accomplished through the labors of a bipartisan delegation, on which such eminent Republicans as Harold Stassen and Arthur Vandenberg were glad to serve and on which, indeed, they served with distinction. On the whole, moreover, the forging of the European policy of the postwar period has not been marred by political maneuvering. The President early appointed a member of the opposition, Senator Austin, to serve as the chief representative of the United States in the

Security Council of the United Nations. Senator Vandenberg, much to the good fortune of the nation, played a part in the negotiation of the peace treaties with the satellite states. When the President came before Congress in 1947 with a request for aid to Greece and Turkey, he received substantial support from the Republican side in both houses (though not so much from the Republicans as from the Democrats). The carrying out of the Marshall Plan showed again that it was possible to base a foreign policy on something more than blind loyalty to the administration.

The epoch-making North Atlantic Defense Treaty of 1949 was ratified by the Senate by a vote of 82 to 13, and American support of the European defense arrangements brought about in 1952 was overwhelming. In the eight years of the Eisenhower administration, though most of the time Congress was in the hands of the Democrats, unstinted backing was given to the chief executive in the European field. Only in the election of 1952 did the partisan spirit obtrude—when the Republicans, or some of them, playing for the votes of citizens of Eastern European background, talked of "rolling back the iron curtain," a promise which encouraged vain hopes in East Germany and Hungary and which was certain not to be kept.

With regard to the East the situation has been somewhat different. The victory of the Communists in China (however much it may have been due to the errors of Chiang Kai-shek) naturally produced a mood of frustration in the United States, of which some members of the Republican Party were quick to take advantage. There followed an unhappy era, in which Senator Joseph McCarthy launched a vicious attack upon the administration, as one riddled with Communists and as one which had, by its ineptitude, sacrificed the interests of the United States in the East. The

witch hunts with which his name will be associated historically had an obviously partisan purpose, though no
doubt extending beyond the Republican organization. In
time, however, Senator McCarthy overreached himself, and
after his censure by the Senate in 1954 his influence declined. Moreover, by the time that the Eisenhower administration had been in power for a little while, a national
consensus was developing with regard to our policy in the
Far East. That policy—alliance with Chiang Kai-shek and
a firm resolve not to recognize the Chinese Communist
regime or approve its admission into the United Nations—
has been much criticized abroad and was not without its
critics at home. But there can be no doubt that the great
weight of opinion approved of the course of the President
and his advisers. At any rate, it came in for very little
criticism from the Democrats in either house of Congress.

Today bipartisanship seems more firmly rooted than
ever before. The issues of foreign policy have become so
grave and so far-reaching that the case for national unity
in the face of a continued and determined rival is very
strong. Undoubtedly, in the last ten years the habit of
bipartisan action in the field of foreign affairs has been
stronger than ever before. The impressive votes given to
President Eisenhower when he asked for authority to use
American forces in Lebanon and in the Far East were
characteristic, not exceptional.

This is not to say that the partisan spirit has been or
can be entirely exorcised. In particular, it is likely to crop
up in the midst of a Presidential campaign, where, inevitably, political calculations assume central importance,
and when, amidst the excitement of the struggle, there is
ample room for indiscretion or even demagoguery. Yet
even here, if we take 1956 and 1960 as examples, the amaz-

ing thing was not the excess, but the control, of the partisan spirit. Only a very deep and genuine division in the field of foreign policy would today find expression in partisan terms. This, it seems to me, is as it should be.

Nonetheless, one hears voices raised from time to time declaring that this lessening of partisan tension is not truly advantageous, and that it tends to an obscuring of issues which ought to be debated in the general interests of democracy and of the American people.

It would certainly be possible to overestimate the damage done by the partisan spirit to the conduct of American foreign policy in the past. However the Federalists acted in 1812–14 and the Whigs in 1846–48, the country came out of the second war with Britain with its position unimpaired and out of the Mexican War with scintillating victories. Throughout the nineteenth century, in fact, it would be difficult to point to any occasion on which political maneuvering seriously damaged the interests of the United States. At the close of the period, Democratic opposition to the "imperialism" of the McKinley administration has usually been charitably judged or actually praised. It is not until the days of the Treaty of Versailles that one meets with a display of factiousness which, however the case for one side or other be stated, certainly was connected with a narrow and intransigent nationalism. Yet even in this case one may wonder whether the partisan debate, unedifying as it often was, was not connected with a very genuine reluctance on the part of the American people to undertake the large role that Woodrow Wilson had marked out for them and whether, had the results of the immediate contest been otherwise, this same reluctance would not have hampered any administration in putting into practice in a bold and fruitful way the principles for which the President was then contending.

In pointing to the record, those who now criticize the bipartisan conception of foreign policy, or the "unpartisan" attitude, as Senator Vandenberg preferred to call it, lay emphasis on the necessity for the discussion of great public issues and the danger of smothering debate by an agreement between the administration and the opposition. They can say, with some reason, that it is desirable that minority opinions get themselves represented in a democracy and that the minority be heard. It is surely the very essence of the democratic process that both sides of all important questions should be presented, and it would be unfortunate if some kind of artificial unity existed among the political leaders, in advance of the development of public opinion. The minority often performs, in foreign affairs as elsewhere, so the argument runs, a useful purpose in criticizing and analyzing policies that are in process of formation, in correcting errors when they are made, and in preventing rash and reckless action in opposition to the national interest. The way to decide a great public issue, it is contended, is to ventilate it thoroughly, to submit it to the test of public approval in a great referendum, and then to abide by the result.

Such a thesis has, from an idealistic point of view, a great deal to be said for it. And indeed, regarding the question practically, those who support the new concept of bipartisanship are not likely to take the position that all differences of opinion should be suppressed in the name of an effective foreign policy. There is, certainly, no chance of this happening in America, and it would be a calamity if it did happen. Bipartisanship, in essence, ought to mean something else. It means, fundamentally, that the administration in power will seek to consult the opposition in advance of the formulation of important principles and will, in the grave matters of diplomacy, admit the minority to a share in the making of decisions in the formulation of policy and in the execution of these decisions. Stated in this way, the principle of bipartisanship is fundamentally sound. It is all very well to talk of debate, but partisan debate, debate carried on as a kind of political maneuvering, is not very likely to be illuminating. Woodrow Wilson in 1920, by his own choice, made the issue of the League of Nations the paramount issue of the political campaign. What happened in practice? Certainly not any very great clarification of the public mind. On the contrary, the whole question became involved in a fog of ambiguities, in a tangle of nationalistic emotion, and in a mass of irrelevant domestic problems. Nobody knows today what the American public really thought of the League when the election was over. What happened on this occasion is only too typical of what is likely to happen if matters of foreign policy become a subject of electoral controversy. Bipartisanship, on the scale in which it is now being practiced in the United States, affords some kind of guarantee against such excesses.

Our discussion of the partisan motif in American diplomacy leads us out of the sphere of congressional politics and into the consideration of the role of public opinion in the shaping of policy. For the introduction of party argument and discussion is an appeal to the prejudices and aspirations and instincts of the electorate. Politicians in the United States, in foreign affairs as in other matters, naturally seek to strengthen their position with the voters. They will not leave these problems to the diplomats. They insist upon having a hand in them. And the American people wish them to do just this.

We have already emphasized, in an earlier chapter, that much of American foreign policy comes up from the people, and we have shown how moralistic considerations and broad principles influence profoundly the American course of action. But we may well call attention here to some of the larger aspects of this question of public opinion and its influence upon American diplomatic practice.

Take the question of secrecy. It is not only in dislike of diplomatic deals, as indicated earlier, that the distrust of leaving decisions to the professionals is indicated. There has been a dislike of secrecy in general. Take, for example, the early practice of considering treaties in executive session in the Senate and, therefore, of treating them as secret documents. Even in the early days of our history there were important breaches of the general rule. One of the very first important international compacts, the Jay Treaty with Great Britain, was, through the calculated indiscretion of a senator, made available in the public press. The principal provisions of the Florida Treaty of February 22, 1819 were stated in Niles's *Register* only five days after the treaty was concluded. The terms of the Ashburton Treaty of 1842, and of the Texas Treaty of 1844, were known before the Senate had acted. In fact, it is hardly too much to say that, in the case of the most important compacts signed by the executive, the rule of secrecy was more honored in the breach than in the observance, and, after 1919, the practice of considering treaties in executive session fell more and more into desuetude. The Treaty of Versailles was debated publicly, and so, too, were the treaties with Germany, Austria, and Hungary, and the series of compacts originated in the Washington Arms

Conference of 1921–22. The pressure, indeed, for a continuation of this practice was so great that on June 18, 1929, by a vote of 60 to 5, the Senate amended its rules to provide that thereafter all treaties would be discussed in open session unless the Senate otherwise decided by a majority vote. While, on occasion, such votes of secrecy have been passed, the overwhelming practice for the last twenty years has been the other way.

In addition to this, the Senate has more and more fallen into the practice of holding hearings on important international accords. The hearings on the Treaty of Versailles lasted for weeks, and produced a truly astounding amount of information and misinformation with regard to that document. There were prolonged hearings on the satellite treaties at the end of the Second World War. Speaking generally, then, the whole set of recent procedure has been to afford the people of the United States a chance to express themselves and to make up their own minds with regard to the major actions of their government in the field of diplomacy.

There are other ways in which the dislike of secrecy has manifested itself in the evolution of American foreign policy. We do not need to concern ourselves in detail with the publication by the government of large amounts of foreign correspondence *after* the event. Yet the bulk of materials presented to the citizen in the United States have always been great as compared with those put forth in any other nation. This was true even in the early days of the government. And, ever since 1861, the State Department has published volumes of diplomatic correspondence and, while these volumes have tended since the First World War to fall behind the actual course of affairs, they are an important indication of the general point of view. More important is the growing custom, inaugurated on a large scale by the Wilson administration, of giving wide currency to negotiations of significance while these negotiations are actually in progress. The notes to Germany on the submarine question, for example, were made available at the very outset of that great controversy. So, too, was no small part of our correspondence with Great Britain. The series of brilliant diplomatic despatches which preceded the armistice agreement of November 1918 were all given to the press, together with the replies of the government of the Reich. There was much information given to the public in connection with the naval disarmament negotiations of 1921–22. In the course of the last forty years, indeed, the trend towards open diplomacy has been nothing short of remarkable, and the debates in the principal agencies of the United Nations have enjoyed the widest currency. There can be little doubt that this tendency will be continued.

One of the factors leading to this result is the increased interest of the press in foreign affairs and its growing insistence on being informed. Newspaper men are not generally much impressed with the necessity of secrecy in diplomatic negotiations. At the peace conference in Paris in 1919 they played a large role and made it extremely difficult to keep from the public news of what was going on. And it was almost inevitable that, as foreign affairs held more and more public attention, there should be an increasing activity on the part of the journalists. This is not to say that all discussions in the field of diplomacy are now conducted in a goldfish bowl. On occasion it has been possible to act in a more traditional manner, and it would not be just to the press itself to say that it has been unwilling to practice restraint when restraint seems most necessary. But there can be little question that a remarkable change has taken place in the last fifty years. The writer was once assured by a distinguished diplomat that he could generally tell what would be the nature of his instructions by reading the despatches in the *New York Times!* This is obviously a far cry from the traditions of the nineteenth century.

This question of secrecy raises some very large problems with regard to the diplomacy of a democratic nation. In discussing it, we must begin by recognizing the fact that it is quite impossible to conduct the foreign affairs of a democracy without informing the mass of the people as to the objectives which the government has in view. In the broad sense, the people have a right to know and will, indeed, insist on knowing. We must recognize, too, that to keep a secret is much more difficult under popular government than it is in a totalitarian state. And, a third important point, it is obvious that the confusion of tongues that results from public debate may give to one's opponent a very false impression of the unity that may underlie the discussion itself. The government of Hitler did not think that the United States would fight; the government of the Soviet Union made a similar miscalculation at the time of the Korean War. The Americans who always clamor for peace, or declare that we must never use the nuclear weapons which we now possess unless they are used against us, however noble their moral convictions, do not make easier the task of those who conduct affairs in Washington. Force is still a major factor in international relations, and to declare that one will not use it is to cripple oneself in advance.

Yet we must not exaggerate the scope of the problem. In time of war it has been possible for democracies to impose very substantial restraints on discussion, and there are signs that in a period of international tension such as the present some degree of secrecy can be effectively maintained. Few people knew about the U-2 (the reconnaissance plane which plotted the Russian defenses) until the plane went down on Russian territory. American encouragement and support of the anti-Castro Cubans received little notice in the press before the actual attack. There seem to be, and doubtless are, more off-the-record discussions in contemporary diplomacy than most of us realize.

It is often said that the diplomacy of a democratic nation tends to rigidity, to the adoption of strong positions based on moral principle, from which retreat is difficult. There is some force in this point of view. Yet are the rigidities of a popular regime any greater than those of a Communist state, encased as it is in its own dogma, its leaders all too often fed only the information they want to hear? As a matter of fact, were we to survey the record of American foreign policy as a whole, we would find many instances of successful retreat from fixed positions where the exigencies of practical life required such action.

It would, in fact, be truer to say that the major difficulty in a democratic foreign policy lies in the tendency to temporize, to wait upon the crystallization of opinion, rather than to lead it, to produce an impression of irresolution. In domestic matters such tactics are often wise, and a nice adjustment of interests through compromise seems the best possible course. But in foreign affairs many questions arise on which one must say flatly yes or no, and decisions have to be taken promptly to be effective. Perhaps the best thing that can be said about the American democracy with regard to this matter is that prompt decision is more and more recognized to be necessary and is, indeed, more common as the exigencies of our age require it.

It is also often maintained, and with reason, that popular diplomacy is based upon emotion, rather than upon cool calculation. The comment is true. We speak of "public opinion." The phrase suggests what the eighteenth-century faith with regard to the democratic process prescribed: that the average man makes up his mind by a purely rational process, by a study of the facts as they are laid before him. No doubt this is an illusion. The facts in any large diplomatic question are often extremely complicated and are, for that matter, even when known, likely to be weighed subjectively. In the case of large groups of people, it might be better to speak of public sentiment rather than of public opinion. For precise and detailed knowledge is not in the possession of the average citizen. His mood and his prejudices are as important as his considered judgments. Indeed, they may influence policy more deeply.

But we must not be too much depressed by this fact. The nondemocratic states suffer from the same fundamental difficulty, from the conflict between disciplined intelligence and unreasoning passion. When we think of Hitler in his bunker, ending that sinister life of his with suicide, of Mussolini in the hands of the mob, of the Japanese warlords beaten to their knees, of the gross miscalculations of Stalin (exposed in the famous speech of February 1956 by Khrushchev himself), we may comfort ourselves with the thought that the errors that spring from popular feeling are less monumental than those committed by totalitarian rulers. Error is natural to man. The record of the democracies in foreign affairs, no matter what the mistakes, seems to me when closely viewed to be at least as good as that of the absolutisms of today.

But however we analyze the problem of open diplomacy, of one thing we may be sure: open diplomacy is here for a long time to come. All sophisticated governments, and some not so sophisticated, attempt to rally the masses behind their foreign policy. The appeal to public opinion may be crude, even false, but it will be there. The existence of the United Nations has opened a new field to diplomats; in that forum there is bound to be a competition for the minds of men, a competition that involves international debate on a grand scale. The representatives of the democracies and of the totalitarian states alike recognize the importance of the struggle that takes place there; and even if we disapproved of this new type of diplomacy, we could not exorcise it.

There is one other aspect of the role of public opinion in foreign policy that ought to be considered here: the effect produced by racial and religious affinities. For years, for example, Irish-American citizens had an active dislike of Great Britain, which inevitably exercised a certain influence on policy, as in connection with the Anglo-American treaties of arbitration of 1897, in the period of neutrality in the First World War, and in the debates on the Treaty of Versailles. In the years 1914–17, the German-Americans were likely to sympathize with the Central Powers, and it was wise statesmanship on the part of Woodrow Wilson to take account of this fact and to see to it that the issue was made clear before the United States entered the conflict. In recent years American Jews have felt strongly about Zionism. It was not possible for the American government, in dealing with the question of war in the Near East, to take precisely the stand in support of the United Nations which it took in Korea. The Polish-Americans have been, quite naturally, among the most vociferous critics of any policy of appeasement of Russia. And to turn to the field of religion, American Catholics have, on the whole, been more sympathetic with General Franco than the mass of Americans, and have felt a strong emotional repugnance to Communism which puts them in the forefront of the foes of the Kremlin. To take another case, many religious-minded people in America through their interest in foreign missions have come to take a romantic interest in China and were, in the years 1937–41, strongly opposed to any concessions to Japan. Congressmen, above all others, take account of these sentiments. Indeed, the catering to these various groups, and the speeches made with this in view, are often embarrassing to those who are charged with the execution of policy and are, too, often misunderstood abroad.

The final conclusion to which this chapter leads is that a democratic foreign policy is a complex business. In a difficult period, it will test more fully than ever before the quality of American public men and the stamina of the American people. We turn, therefore, in the final chapter of this book to the secular struggle between the democratic states and the forces of Communism, which is one of the salient facts of the international situation today.

X

The Secular Struggle

I N the opening chapter of this book, we sought to trace the development of American foreign policy from its beginnings to 1945. In that long period momentous changes took place, changes which marked the rise of the United States from a provincial nation, preoccupied with the affairs of the North American continent, or, at most, of the two Americas, to the status of a world power. But the year 1945 may well mark a new dividing line in the study of American diplomacy; for the end of the Second World War created a wholly new situation. The power of militarist Germany and of militarist Japan had been broken; but no secure peace emerged as a result. On the contrary, the struggle left behind two powers of portentous strength, two powers with conflicting ideologies, conflicting ambitions, and indeed conflicting dreams as to the nature of the world society of the future. To say this is not to discount entirely or to rule out of the account the role of other states, of Britain, of France, of Germany, on the one hand, of the Chinese People's Republic, on the other; but it is obvious that no state can exercise in the immediate future the weight in international affairs that is exercised by the United States and the Soviet Union. No study of American foreign policy would be complete which did not measure the significance of this new alignment and seek to estimate the forces at work in the world of today.

It is fair to say that while the Second World War was still being fought, a great many Americans were disposed to believe in the possibility of an understanding with the colossus of the Kremlin. The war itself had brought together the Soviet Union and the United States as allies; the dramatic meeting of the great war leaders at Teheran at the end of 1943 seemed to augur well for the future; and the conference at Yalta in 1945, whatever may be the judgment of it today, was at the time almost universally hailed as a confirmation of that unity which had been affirmed and consolidated in the capital of Iran. There is a limit to the value of polls of public opinion; but it is surely of some significance that, in March of 1945, more than half of those interrogated on the possibilities of cooperation with Russia at the end of the war took the optimistic view, and that out of the full 100 percent polled, making allowances for the 14 percent who remained undecided, the vote was almost two to one in favor of this hopeful judgment of the future.

We can readily see why this was true. The whole nature of the American system of government lays the emphasis on compromise, and this emphasis is powerfully reinforced by the success which the American people have had in operating a democratic system. At the end of the war their instincts, the deep-seated and noble instincts of a great self-governing people, led them to the view that human differences are usually capable of adjustment, that somehow a compromise could be found between the ideals and interests of their own society and the ideals and interests of another. While they had learned something of the importance of force in the affairs of men, they still hoped for and valued peace. They were able, as their history has shown, to assume that they were themselves capable of error and that these errors might be and ought to be corrected. They possessed faith, a faith often demonstrated in the democratic process, but not a faith so absolute that it made them desirous of imposing, without ruth or scruple, their own system on the whole world. They looked forward, as they have looked forward after every war, to a long period of tranquillity. Characteristically, they viewed with complacency the immense reduction of American military power which followed on the end of the conflict; they began to talk of economy and, though in a different context from that of 1920, of a return to normalcy.

The hopeful temper of the American people was reflected in the diplomacy of 1945 and in the policies of Roosevelt and Truman. There were, before Roosevelt died, some important instances of friction between Washington and Moscow, and at least one which irritated the President extremely; but in one of the last letters he ever wrote, he expressed himself to Winston Churchill as of the opinion that the difficulties which constantly arose seemed to "straighten out." Moreover, Roosevelt's course of action in his last months of office was based quite definitely on the hypothesis that Russian good will could be had at a price. At Yalta he consented, apparently without great difficulty, to the idea of three votes for the Soviet Union in the Assembly of the projected United Nations, though there existed no sound legal ground for such a concession; he bargained for Russian support in the war against Japan, by agreeing to the restoration of Russian privileges in Manchuria, and to the acquisition by the Soviet Union of Sakhalin and the Kuriles; and in considering the problem of Eastern Europe, he acted on the assumption that governments could be constituted there in which Communists would be represented side by side with other political groups, and play their part in a truly democratic evolution of the peoples concerned; and he encouraged the Russians to hope for a sympathetic consideration of the problem of reparations. The situation was not much changed by his death. For a substantial period the hope of an understanding with the Kremlin continued to persist, at least in some degree. The mission of Harry Hopkins to Moscow in June 1945 ended with an understanding with Stalin on an important aspect of the problem of the United Nations charter. The conference at Potsdam sought to work out a formula for reparations which would be regardful of Russian interests, and which actually conceded deliveries from the West to the East. The Truman administration put forward the idea of a twenty-five-year alliance to prevent the recurrence of German aggression, obviously with the idea that the Kremlin might be quieted in its fears by such a compact. The question of the atomic bomb was handled in such a manner as to suggest that the United States would renounce this weapon under proper guarantees. The American government continued to hope and to press for the organization of regimes in Eastern Europe and the Balkans in which Communists and other elements would cooperate. In all these matters, looking at the matter from the American point of view, a spirit of conciliation was evident.

On the other hand, we must not underestimate the factors which made for antagonism toward the Soviet Union. The Communist system was certainly a challenge to the economic order of the West and could hardly fail to arouse a deep hostility in many of those who were devoted to that order. Businessmen and men of property especially might be expected to find in the doctrines and ambitions of the Kremlin a deadly menace, and might react emotionally in very emphatic fashion against them. There were those, too, who had long looked with bitter hostility upon Russia as the enemy of religion. In particular, this was true of much of the Catholic population of the United States, though this feeling was not confined solely to Catholics. Marxian materialism, to many persons, seemed a threat both to the ideals and to the vested interests of the church, and a somewhat increasing tolerance of religious observance in the Soviet Union did not alter the just conviction that religion in Russia was not free and, at best, was little more than the subservient tool of an all-powerful state.

But there was still a third factor to take into account. Americans of the right were often joined by Americans of the left in dislike of the Russian regime. The question, after all, was one of proportion. It might be true that the welfare of the masses was the objective of the men in the Kremlin (though even this might be debated); but, granted that this was so, was it worth the price of a bloody tyranny that used the concentration camp and the secret police to maintain itself in power, that prostituted the human mind to the necessities of Marxist dogmatism, that was cynically disregardful of any standard of truth in dealing with the outside world, and that was capable, as experience had shown in 1939, of the most shameless kind of diplomatic bargaining with those who menaced the peace of the world? From a point of view very different from that of the conservatives, these people were conditioned in 1945 towards increasing dislike of Soviet policy.

In addition to all this, there was one other factor to be

considered. The centrifugal tendencies in international affairs have almost always affirmed themselves at the end of a great war. Once the peril which menaced both the Soviet Union and the United States had been banished, it was natural that each government should think first of its own interests and its own aspirations. And these interests and aspirations were, after all, fundamentally different. The leaders in the Kremlin looked forward naturally enough to a Communist world, to the spread of their political and economic system, and were little concerned with the tasks of peace and reconstruction within the context of an existing order. The United States, on the other hand, hoped for a Europe restored to tranquillity within the fabric of the familiar democratic ideal; it wished to see economic recovery rather than drastic modification of existing institutions; and it therefore set a high value on recovery. With such divergent interests and aspirations it is probable that a conflict of views was more or less inevitable.

It is really not a fruitful subject of investigation to examine as to which side provoked whom. There were no doubt some grounds for resentment of American policy on the part of the Kremlin. For example, the abrupt termination of Lend-Lease at the end of the German war was naturally highly irritating to Moscow. To the Soviet Union, the interest of the United States in Eastern Europe seemed an officious interference in what might be regarded as a Russian security zone. The extremely attenuated role given to powers other than America in the regulation of the affairs of Japan after the surrender of September 1945, the treatment of the Soviet representatives as "articles of furniture," in Stalin's phrase, could hardly make for international harmony. The speech of Winston

Churchill at Fulton, Missouri, in February of 1946, in which he virtually proposed united Anglo-American action to contain the ambitions of the government at Moscow, naturally produced violent repercussions. The support of Iran in its demand for the withdrawal of Russian troops from its soil, though fully justified by previous agreements and the Charter of the United Nations, could hardly be expected to produce delight in the breast of Molotov or Stalin.

But the complaints could hardly have been all on one side. As early as February of 1945, on the heels of the Yalta conference, Vishinsky appeared at Bucharest and forced upon the Rumanians a government that, in its composition, gave the clearest evidence of the intent to communize the country. In the same month as Potsdam, the Soviet Union began to attack the policy of the Western powers in Greece, put in a preposterous demand for a trusteeship in the Mediterranean, fixed the frontier between Poland and East Germany by unilateral action, placed what had once been German territory under Polish administration without consulting its Allies, exerted pressure upon Turkey for the control of the Dardanelles, and, in violation of ordinary practice, began to remove large amounts of machinery and other movables from East Germany as reparations. In September, Molotov, against the opposition of the Western powers, broke up the Council of Foreign Ministers on a question of procedure. In December, there were signs that the Russians were supporting an autonomist movement in northern Iran. Clearly, the Soviet Union was not going to be easy to deal with in the building of the new world order.

But it is not the object of this chapter to narrate in detail the story of the deterioration of Russo-American relations. There is good reason to believe that shortly after Yalta the whole question of such relations was thoroughly and cold-bloodedly examined by the Politburo, and that the decision was taken to pursue an aggressive rather than a conciliatory policy towards the United States, that it was reckoned, in strict accord with Marxist dialectics, that the end of the war would be followed by an economic crisis in America and, naturally, in Europe, and that it would not be long before the Communist cause would triumph. Certainly the course of Russian policy in the next few years was to produce progressive disillusionment among the Americans who hoped for understanding. The gradual tightening of Russian control in Eastern Europe, the opposition of the Kremlin to the American proposals for economic recovery that took shape in the Marshall Plan, the encouragement given to the Greek guerrillas, the difficulties thrown in the way of the organization of a united Germany, the encouragement given to disorder in Western Europe, the blockade of Berlin—these and many other actions could hardly fail to produce a profound reaction in the United States or to produce their repercussions on American policy. And it is significant that in the evolution of an American answer to Russia the partisan note was reduced to a minimum. It was, as we have seen, a Republican Congress which extended aid to Greece and Turkey in 1947 and which endorsed the Marshall Plan with its wide program for recovery; it was through the action of both parties that there was brought into being in 1949 the Atlantic Pact for the defense of Western Europe; there was strong biparty support for the program of arms aid that followed.

From the signing of the North Atlantic Treaty to our own day, that instrument has formed the basis of American policy in Europe. Though there have been strains and inadequacies in the operation of the alliance, it remains intact. It has behind it the overwhelming weight of American opinion and of European opinion as well. It stands as a bulwark against direct Russian aggression. At the moment of writing it is being tested by the thorny controversy over free Berlin. How it will withstand this test is, of course, a speculative matter, but, as has happened before, Russian bluster tends to solidify it. Of course it is true that the situation in Western Europe is not the ideal one. The West and the Kremlin distrust each other and seek different goals. Twice in the last decade, attempts have been made to reduce the tension by conversations at the Summit. The idea has been widely held, and it is a tempting idea, that if the leaders of the West and the Russians might only talk with one another, their difficulties and antagonisms might be resolved. The facts have not borne out this view. The Geneva conference of 1955, in which Eisenhower and Khrushchev met face to face, resulted in no advance whatever. In 1960 the second Geneva conference lasted but a single day, breaking up when the forced landing of an American reconnaissance plane on Russian territory afforded the Russian leader a pretext or a reason for sabotaging a meeting from which it was clear no great results were to be expected. At the moment of writing there seems no good reason to believe that the two great rivals will desist from their rivalry. Indeed, since Russian power, relative to the United States, has grown rather than declined since 1949, the chances of a general settlement have diminished rather than increased.

The year 1949, the year of the Atlantic Pact, marks two other important changes in the status of American foreign relations. It is the year in which the Russians exploded their first atomic bomb, and it was followed by the explosion of a hydrogen bomb four years later. The advantage of terror, of "massive retaliation," as John Foster Dulles put it, which the United States enjoyed in the first years after the war had been lost. Today the two great protagonists possess the capacity for mutual destruction. What this means, or may mean in practice, we shall have occasion to examine a little later.

The year 1949 also saw the triumph of the Communists in China. To the portentous power of the Kremlin was now added the power of the most populous nation in the world. Nor was it long before this power was exerted. In the war in Korea initiated in 1950, the Chinese Communists soon intervened. In opposition to this new threat, the years after 1950 saw an American attempt to consolidate the position in Asia, as it had been already consolidated in Europe. A commitment in Korea was followed by a treaty by which the United States and Japan were brought into close association, by a treaty of alliance with Chiang Kai-shek on his island refuge in Formosa, by the pact of Manila which associated France, Great Britain, Australia, New Zealand, Thailand, and the Philippines in mutual defense of their territories, and by the support of a non-Communist government in South Vietnam. None of these compacts contained pledges quite so categorical as those embodied in the North Atlantic Treaty. But all suggested that in the East, as in Europe, the United States would oppose aggression.

In the Middle East the situation was somewhat different. The United States smiled upon, but did not sign, the so-called Baghdad Pact, originally agreed to by Great Britain, Turkey, Iran, Iraq, and Pakistan, and now, as the Central Treaty Organization, still in existence (Iraq having withdrawn). Thus a whole network of understandings has been constructed to discourage direct aggression on the part of the Soviet Union.

The value and durability of these various commitments may well vary. All such associations exhibit centrifugal tendencies, and we may be sure that Russian diplomacy will be active, by cajolery, intimidation, or subversion, to undermine them when it can. But it ought not to be thought that they are useless.

With regard to the situation on the continent of Asia, it may well be that the United States would hesitate before committing ground troops as it did in Korea. But it can and does assist in the strengthening of local forces which can withstand external attack or internal subversion. And up to the moment of writing there has been no such attack either on Korea or on South Vietnam.

With regard to the island territories of the Pacific, the situation is different. There, for the present, the power of the United States dominates, and a challenge to it is not imminent. It is true that the Chinese Communists in 1955 and 1958 bombarded the coastal islands of Quemoy and Matsu, held by the Nationalists, but these islands were not included in specific terms in the treaty with Chiang, and the fact that no all-out attack on Formosa has ever been made testifies to the value of the American pledge. An attack on Japan or on the Philippines is a most remote contingency.

In the Middle East, the United States, as already stated, is less committed. Yet here in 1958 took place one of the most striking events of the decade from the point of view of American policy. An unsettled situation in Lebanon (contemporaneous with a revolution in Iraq and troubles in Jordan) led the Lebanese government to call upon the American government to assist in the preservation of order.

Marines were landed and the situation stabilized. Roars of rage came from the Kremlin, but the roars were unaccompanied by action. The episode is of the first importance. It seems to suggest that resolute action by the United States to come to the aid of a regime which asks for support against internal troubles will not be likely to produce intervention by the Soviet Union.

Yet American armed action in other states can be risky business, both in terms of the image of the United States that it presents and in terms of the commitments to which it gives rise. It does not appear that this is at all likely to be the usual pattern in the competition of the Russians and the Americans for a favored position in the less developed nations of the world.

We come, then, to a fundamental aspect of the Russian-American competition of power. Russian policy seems to be tending towards subversion and encouragement of social unrest rather than in the direction of conquest. Will it be their system or ours in those numerous parts of the world where the future is being made in patterns very different from those of the past? It is undeniable that the Kremlin has many cards in its hands in those large areas of the world where the old order is crumbling and a new one being born. Colonialism is a dying phenomenon, and its decay leaves the great nations of the West on the defensive. The services performed by "imperialist" powers are minimized or denied, and the young liberated peoples demand full recognition of their independence and equal status. The gross social and economic inequalities that exist in many countries (not necessarily all of them former colonies), in Latin America, in the Middle East, in Asia, provide a fertile field for troublemaking and for the growth of Communism. The sensational exploits of the Russians in the industrial field, exploits effectively dramatized, create in new communities seeking industrialization the conviction (or, at least, assumption) that the Russian way may be the best way to forge a modern state. The display of Russian power, the sputniks and the astronauts, produce a similar effect. Finally, the color problem operates to diminish the influence of the West among the nonwhite peoples emerging into freedom.

We shall, indeed, have to go further. It is exceedingly doubtful whether the political system of the West is susceptible of imitation in many of the new states—or indeed in all of the old ones. Democracy is a tender plant, at best. Historically it has thrived only where property is widely distributed, where habits of legality have taken deep root, where the instinct for compromise and adjustment has been strong. What works in Western Europe or in North America or in some Latin American states may not work at all in the Middle East, or in Asia, or in Africa.

But this does not mean, it need not mean, that the nations which are not democratic will inevitably become the slaves of the Kremlin. The strongest force of our time, one far stronger than Communism, is nationalism. This may well mean that the various societies of the contemporary world will shape their own future in terms of their own needs, social systems, and national temperaments. Communism itself shows signs of variety—the Yugoslav version, the Polish version, the Russian version, the Chinese version— and the differences are more likely to become greater than to disappear. Nor is it necessarily the case that states nondemocratic in form will be Communist in economic policy. Most of the communities outside the Soviet sphere are tied to the West by their economic relations, such as the oil-producing states of the Middle East which have every interest in maintaining some viable relationship with those who buy their product, or the raw-material-producing countries of Latin America which sell principally to the United States and, secondarily, to Europe. Most of these communities need external capital, public capital and private capital both, if they can get it on reasonable terms. An attempt to interfere with their development on the part of the Kremlin may very well, in due course, as the sinister and selfish nature of Russian policy becomes apparent, prove self-defeating.

But what does all this mean in terms of American policy? What are the objectives to be aimed at? How are they to be sought? By what means, in this competition we have just examined, will American policy seek to further its ends? What is the American consensus with regard to foreign policy today?

In the first place, Americans have reluctantly come to recognize the role of power in international affairs. They do not intend to divest themselves of power. The course of the last ten years clearly indicates this. To act otherwise, they realize, is to run the risk of submitting to endless intimidation. This they have no mind to do.

In the second place (and here again the record is clear), they intend, by a policy of economic assistance to less developed nations, to strengthen these nations against the Communist menace. Since the initiation of the Marshall Plan, they have spent billions of dollars with this end in view. The national consensus has been formed. There is no sign that it will be shaken. The effectiveness of such a policy will doubtless vary with time and circumstance; the circumstances for its application, it must be frankly stated, are not as favorable as they were in Europe, where there existed a disposition to united action, a genuine sense of fiscal responsibility and a desire to balance the national budget, and an immediate and widespread fear of Communism. But the chances by no means run wholly against the United States. The Russians make many mistakes in the field of economic policy and it is possible to capitalize on these.

In the third place, Americans look sympathetically upon international collaboration through the agency of the United Nations. They have, in the last fifteen years, brought forward many proposals to strengthen that collaboration, for example, the Acheson-Baruch-Lilienthal Plan for the control of atomic energy and the International Atomic Energy Commission. They have supported the United Nations in setting up an international force in the Gaza strip, after the unhappy war between Egypt and France, Great Britain, and Israel. They have supported the United Nations in its efforts to bring peace to the troubled Congo.

In the fourth place, Americans desire a reduction of armaments, if this is compatible with the national security. They have demonstrated this from the time of the Acheson-Baruch-Lilienthal Plan thenceforward. It is not they, but the Russians, who initiated the portentous competition of armaments which exists in the world today. They have been ready to suspend nuclear testing under proper guarantees. It is the Russians, not they, who broke the truce with regard to this matter.

In the fifth place, they seek to keep open the channels of trade and the channels of information. Although there are deviations and weaknesses in the record, the American government stands for development of wide international trade and wide exchange of ideas, in the belief that both strengthen the kind of society in which it believes.

No man can foresee the future. No man can predict success for the policy of any nation, nor can any nation, however powerful, hope by itself to shape the destiny of the human race. But in the objectives that they propose to themselves, the American people seem to be seeking a better and more peaceful era for the world at large.

Bibliographical Note

THERE is, of course, a vast literature on American foreign policy. *Harvard Guide to American History*, edited by Oscar Handlin and others (1954), is the best bibliographical aid, down to 1954. See also, for a less comprehensive view, T. A. Bailey, *A Diplomatic History of the American People* (5th ed., 1955).

Standard texts on American diplomatic history are Samuel Flagg Bemis, *A Diplomatic History of the United States* (4th ed., 1955), J. W. Pratt, *A History of United States Foreign Policy* (1955), and Bailey, *A Diplomatic History of the American People*. An interesting topical treatment of American foreign policy is Richard W. Van Alstyne, *American Diplomacy in Action* (1944). A summary of our policy in the Far East for the period 1898–1937 is A. Whitney Griswold, *The Far Eastern Policy of the United States* (1938).

On American imperialism, the best one-volume treatment is by J. W. Pratt, *America's Colonial Experiment* (1950). A more superficial account is that by William H. Haas, *The American Empire* (1940). For special treatments, there are the following: For the Philippines, J. Ralston Hayden and Dean Conant Worcester, *The Philippines, Past and Present* (1930). For Cuba, Russell H. Fitzgibbon, *Cuba and the United States, 1900–1935* (1935), down to the fall of Machado. For Haiti, Arthur C. Mills-paugh, *Haiti under American Control, 1915–1930* (1931). For the Dominican Republic, Melvin Knight, *The Americans in Santo Domingo* (1928). For Nicaragua, I. J. Cox, *Nicaragua and the United States, 1909–1927* (1927). For the Caribbean as a whole, see Dana G. Munro, *The United States and the Caribbean Area* (1934), and Dexter Perkins, *The United States and the Caribbean* (1947). For the retreat from imperialism, see S. F. Bemis, *The Latin American Policy of the United States* (1943), especially chapters 12–16. For postwar policies with regard to Germany and Japan, see the volumes published by the Council on Foreign Relations, *The United States in World Affairs* (1931–).

An excellent treatment of the economic forces in American foreign policy, though perhaps overemphasizing the role of the business class, is B. H. Williams, *Economic Foreign Policy of the United States* (1929). On the role of the financial interests, see J. W. Angell, *Financial Foreign Policy of the United States* (1933). See also, on the financial aspects of Latin American policy down to the Second World War, Willy Feuerlein, *Dollars in Latin America* (1941), an illuminating study. An interesting discussion of the Marxist hypothesis as applied to foreign affairs is to be found in Lionel Robbins, *The Economic Causes of War* (1940). Two works not to be neglected are Quincy Wright, *A Study of War*, 2 vols. (1942) and *The Causes of War and the Conditions of Peace* (1935). There is no general study of the American attitude towards war, though some interesting observations will be found in Wright, *A Study of War*, and a brief philosophical analysis by Dexter Perkins, "The American Attitude towards War," in *Yale Review*, XXXVIII, no. 2 (1949), 234–52.

For individual wars, the most recent account of the diplomacy leading to the War of 1812 is Bradford Perkins, *Prologue to War* (1961). Other works are J. W. Pratt, *Expansionists of 1812* (1925), and, from a very different point of view, A. L. Burt, *The United States, Great Britain and British North America from the Revolution to the Establishment of Peace after the War of 1812* (1940). For the Mexican War, there is Justin H. Smith, *The War with Mexico* (1919), and, less nationalistic, G. L. Rives, *The United States and Mexico, 1821–1848* (1913). For the Spanish-American War, the latest account is Ernest R. May, *Imperial Democracy: The Emergence of the U.S. as a Great Power* (1961). There is also an interesting account by Walter Millis, *The Martial Spirit* (1931), to be used with caution but still the best-rounded narrative. For the First World War, the most recent account consolidating previous narratives is Ernest R. May, *The World War and American Isolation, 1914–1917* (1959). See also Charles Seymour, *American Diplomacy during the World War* (1942), giving the conventional view, Charles Tansill, *America Goes to War* (1938), which is slanted towards revisionism, and E. M. Borchard and W. P. Lage, *Neutrality for the United States* (1940), a militantly revisionist study.

For the approach of the Second World War, an indispensable two-volume work is W. L. Langer and S. E. Gleason, *World Crisis and American Foreign Policy: The Challenge to Isolation, 1937–1940* (1952) and *The Undeclared War, September 1940–December 1941* (1953), which covers the period down to 1941 and traces the evolution of policy which brought the United States into the war. For the same years and the war period itself, the annual surveys of American diplomacy published by the Council on Foreign Relations are of great value. See also

W. H. McNeill, *America, Britain and Russia: Their Co-operation and Conflict* (1953). Finally, the works of Herbert Feis should be consulted, especially *The Road to Pearl Harbor* (1950), *Churchill, Roosevelt and Stalin: The War They Waged and the Peace They Sought* (1957), and *Japan Subdued: The Atomic Bomb and the End of the War in the Pacific* (1961).

On the peace movement in the United States, there is an interesting work by Merle Curti, *Peace or War: The American Struggle, 1636–1936* (1936). For American arbitrations, see J. B. Moore, *The Principles of American Diplomacy* (1918), and, for the Kellogg-Briand Pact, see Robert H. Ferrell, *Peace in Their Time: The Origins of the Kellogg-Briand Pact* (1952). For the series of pacts with Latin America, there is much material in Bemis, *Latin American Policy of the United States*, already cited. On the development of the navy and its relation to American peace sentiments, the best work is H. and M. Sprout, *The Rise of American Naval Power* (1944), and, on the army, W. A. Ganoe, *The History of the United States Army* (1942). See also Walter Millis, *Arms and Men: A Study in American Military History* (1960).

There is a spate of works on the Presidency. But the best is still E. S. Corwin, *The President, Office and Powers, 1787–1948* (1948). On the Secretary of State, see the volume under this title published by the American Assembly (1960), a series of highly interesting essays. On the State Department itself, see James L. McCamy, *The Administration of Foreign Affairs* (1950), and Graham H. Stuart, *The Department of State, a History of Its Organization, Procedure and Personnel* (1949). On the Central Intelligence Agency, the best work is H. H. Ransom, *Central Intelligence and National Security* (1958), and, on the

National Security Council, Paul H. Hammond, *Organizing for Defense: The American Military Establishment in the Twentieth Century* (1961).

For the role of Congress, see the illuminating study by R. A. Dahl, *Congress and Foreign Policy* (1950), and H. Bradford Westerfield, *Foreign Policy and Party Politics* (1955). For the Senate and its place in international relations, three key works exist: W. Stull Holt, *Treaties Defeated in the Senate* (1933), R. J. Dangerfield, *In Defense of the Senate: A Study in Treaty-Making* (1933), and D. H. Fleming, *The Treaty Veto in the American Senate* (1930). For the development of executive agreements, see E. M. Boyd, *Treaties and Executive Agreements in the United States: Their Separate Roles and Limitations* (1960). For the role of public opinion, there is a penetrating study by Gabriel Almond, *The American People and Foreign Policy* (1950).

For the period since 1945, there exists a vast literature. For the whole period, see the volumes in the series edited by the Council on Foreign Relations. For the Stalin period, see George F. Kennan, *Russia and the West under Lenin and Stalin* (1961), and, for the post-Stalin period, David J. Dallin, *Soviet Foreign Policy after Stalin* (1961). For the Korean War there is a valuable work by J. W. Spanier, *The Truman-MacArthur Controversy and the Korean War* (1959). For the Far East, see A. Doak Barnett, *Communist China and Asia: Challenge to American Policy* (1960).

INDEX

INDEX

Capitalism. *See* Economic influences on foreign policy

Caribbean area, U.S. policy in, 34–35, 36–37, 56–60, 82, 109, 144, 202. *See also* Cuba; Dominican Republic; Haiti; Puerto Rico; Virgin Islands

Castro, Fidel, 35, 39, 58, 184, 213

Catholics, American, 216, 221

Central America: U.S. policy in, 7, 43–44, 108–109; Great Britain in, 8, 142. *See also* British Honduras; Costa Rica; Guatemala; Nicaragua; Panama; Panama Canal Zone

Central American nonrecognition agreements (1907, 1923), 46, 56, 82

Central Intelligence Agency, 157, 184–185

Central Treaty Organization, 226

Chapultepec protocol, 113, 203

Chesapeake-Leopard incident, 101

Chiang Kai-shek, 19, 113, 146, 204, 205, 226, 227

Chile, 28

China: pre-Communist, 9, 15–16, 51, 52, 53, 56, 66, 91, 92, 93–94, 115, 216; and Japan, 17, 19, 20, 93–94, 104, 106, 166, 173; Communist, 39, 47, 87, 96, 132, 186, 204, 205, 217, 226, 227, 229. *See also* Far East; Manchuria

Chinese Exclusion Act (1882), 197

Christianity, 120–121

Churchill, Winston, 46, 219, 222–223

Civil liberties, during war, 114–115

Civil War, American, 5, 7, 52, 53, 62, 81, 99, 114, 121, 130, 131, 142, 147

Clark memorandum, 37, 203

Clay, Henry, 79, 141, 202

Clayton-Bullwer Treaty, 62

Cleveland, Grover, 170; administration, 7, 89, 143

Colby, Bainbridge, 86

Collective security, 95, 110–114

Colombia, 28, 90

Communism, 39, 40, 72, 86–87, 115, 145, 204, 213, 216, 220, 221, 222, 224, 226, 228, 229, 230, 231

Congress, U.S., 18, 25, 33, 64, 79, 107, 124, 139, 144, 145, 157, 158, 164, 166, 171, 172, 178, 180, 183, 185, 187, 196–200, 201, 205, 216; tariff, 52, 54; war declarations, 141, 168; money appropriation, 165, 204, 224; joint resolutions, 193–195. *See also* Executive-legislative relations; House of Representatives; Senate

Conscription policy, 26, 131, 172, 202

Constitution, U.S., 2, 32, 121, 157, 161, 167, 191–192, 194

Coolidge, Calvin, 57, 86, 145, 200

Costa Rica, 57

Council of Foreign Bondholders, 61

Council of Foreign Ministers (Four-Power), 223

Court of International Justice, 24

Crimean War, 118

Cuba, 30, 31, 34, 35, 42, 47, 55, 57, 168; and Spanish-American War, 14–15, 101, 102, 104, 105, 106, 123, 143, 169; and Castro, 39, 58, 184, 213

Czechoslovakia, 86

Dangerfield, Royden, 189, 193

Danish West Indies, 14, 31

Danzig, 85

Davis, Norman, 163

Dawes Plan (1924), 24, 60

Declaration of Independence, 32

Defense, Department of, 157, 183, 185

Democratic Party, 53, 90, 111, 144, 181, 202, 204, 205, 206

Democratic Republican Party, 50, 201

Denmark, 85, 165

Depression of 1837, 148, 151

Depression of 1873, 151

INDEX

48, 67, 72, 73, 94, 101, 102, 112,
124, 169, 173; in World War I,
21–22, 25, 27, 64, 65, 92, 101, 102,
105, 110, 112, 124, 169; East, 223
Ghent, Treaty of (1814), 51, 117,
126
Good-neighbor Policy, 182, 203.
See also Latin America
Grant, Ulysses S., 170; administration, 7, 14, 31, 89, 176, 178, 199
Great Britain, 3, 6, 8, 10, 12, 60, 83,
93, 94, 96, 110, 117, 132, 146, 149,
150, 175, 217, 231; War of 1812,
4, 99, 101, 102, 105, 107, 122, 171,
206; Venezuela–British Guiana
dispute, 7, 9, 109, 143; relations
with U.S., 14, 15, 21, 22, 23, 26,
48, 50, 51, 62, 64, 78, 97, 100, 108,
113, 121, 124, 126, 127, 138, 141,
142, 144, 164, 190, 192, 194, 199,
201, 209, 211, 215, 223, 226
Great Lakes neutralization treaty
(1817), 117
Greece, 79, 194, 200, 204, 223, 224
Greenland, occupation of, 26, 165
Greer episode, 124, 168
Guadelupe Hidalgo, Treaty of
(1848), 90
Guam, 15, 17, 31, 34, 41, 112, 132,
169
Guatemala, 40

Habeas corpus, writ of, 114
Hague Conventions (1899, 1907),
4, 126
Haiti, 31, 34, 35, 36, 42, 43, 47, 57,
59–60, 98
Haitian Banque Nationale, 59
Halleck, Charles, 203
Hanna, Mark, 63, 181
Harding, Warren G., 36, 177; ad-
ministration, 17, 24, 86, 178
Harrison, William Henry, 175
Havana conferences: *1928*, 37;
1940, 28
Hawaii, 14, 15, 52, 55, 89, 115, 143,
194
Hawley-Smoot Act (1930), 54, 61

Hay, John, 16, 17, 52, 179, 189
Hayes, Rutherford B., 7
Hay-Pauncefote Treaty, 189–190
Hearst, William Randolph, 14
Herrick, Robert, 110
Hitler, Adolf, 25, 26, 27, 66, 72, 88,
94, 102, 103, 105, 112, 119, 125,
152, 167, 172, 196, 212, 214
Hoover, Herbert, 170, 175; admin-
istration, 18, 19, 145
Hopkins, Harry, 163, 179, 220
House, Col. Edward M., 163, 179
House of Representatives, U.S., 32,
33, 81, 131, 158, 159, 162, 199, 200,
202, 203. *See also* Congress, U.S.
Huerta, Victoriano, 36, 47, 82, 160
Hughes, Charles Evans, 38, 178,
179, 182, 203
Hull, Cordell, 38, 53, 95, 158, 179,
180, 196
Hungary, 80, 92, 97, 142, 195, 204,
209

Iceland, occupation of, 26, 168
Immigration policies, 5, 18, 24, 145
Imperialism, U.S., 27, 29–48, 55, 76,
89, 91, 103, 121, 122, 130, 173, 206
In Defense of the Senate, 189
India, 48
Indian wars, U.S., 98
Indochina, 20
Indonesia, 48
Industrial Revolution, 118
International Atomic Energy Com-
mission, 231
International Bank, 61
International Red Cross, 4
Iran, 146, 223, 226
Iraq, 226, 227
Isolationism, U.S., 1, 2–5, 21, 23, 24,
25, 26, 27, 66, 136, 191
Israel, 96, 231
Italy, 85, 118, 128, 132, 195

Jackson, Andrew, 13, 98, 100, 140,
175; administration, 53, 128, 141,
176, 202
Japan, 51, 91, 115, 143, 166, 175, 190;

{ 242 }

INDEX

INDEX

Maximilian, Archduke, 7, 9, 109
Metternich, Prince von, 80
Mexican War, 11, 13, 30, 90, 99, 101, 102, 103, 104, 123, 130, 141–142, 147, 148, 173, 202, 206
Mexico, 28, 30, 108; and France, 7, 9, 109, 142; relations with U.S., 11, 36, 39, 43, 47, 55, 56, 57, 81, 82, 90, 123, 144, 145, 167, 192
Middle East, 114, 226, 227–228, 229
Military establishment, U.S., 130–134, 219, 231
Millis, Walter, 123
Molotov, Vyacheslav, 223
Monroe, James, 108, 170, 175; administration, 4, 6, 37, 51, 79, 108, 141, 166, 201
Monroe Doctrine, 1, 4, 5–10, 51, 79–80, 108, 140, 141, 166; Roosevelt corollary, 37, 145, 181, 182
Montevideo conference and protocol (1933), 38, 39, 44, 58, 129, 203
Moral influences on U.S. foreign policy, 45, 46–47, 71, 72–97, 105, 106, 129, 156, 209, 212, 213
Morgan, J. P., 69
Morris, Gouverneur, 163, 192
Morrow mission, 203
Mussolini, Benito, 26, 196, 214

Naples, 6
Napoleon Bonaparte, 4; and Louisiana Purchase, 10, 12–13, 99
Napoleon III, 7, 9, 81, 108–109
Napoleonic wars, 5
Nasser, Gamal, 96
National City Bank of New York, 59
National Guard, 130
Nationalism, U.S., 130, 131, 140, 141, 142, 143, 145, 146, 147, 148, 194, 206, 208
National security, U.S., 8, 107–110, 112–113, 116–117, 135, 231
National Security Council, 157, 185–186
National Security League, 110

National Socialism, 84, 94, 106
Near East, 9, 51, 216
Netherlands, 175
Neutrality, U.S., 3, 21, 25, 106, 124, 138, 144, 160, 215
Neutrality Acts, 25, 146, 196
Neutrality Proclamation (1793), 105, 160
New Deal, 38, 54. See also Roosevelt, Franklin D.
Newfoundland, fortification of, 26, 164
New Orleans, 107
New Zealand, 113, 226
Nicaragua, 8, 31, 34, 36, 37, 41, 43, 47, 56, 57, 59, 142
Niles' Register, 209
Nine-Power Treaty (1922), 17, 56
North Atlantic Treaty Organization (1949). See Atlantic Pact
Northwest territory, acquisition of, 10, 99
Nuclear weapons, 133–134, 212, 220, 226, 231

Obregon regime, 56
Office of Civil and Defense Mobilization, 185
Office of Strategic Services, 184
Okinawa, 40
Open-Door Policy, 16, 52, 56
Oregon, 7, 141; treaty of 1846, 12, 161
Organization of American States, 88
Ostend Manifesto, 30

Pakistan, 113, 226
Panama, 31, 34, 35, 40, 90, 141
Panama Canal Zone, 31, 190
Panama congress: 1826, 8, 201; 1939, 28
Pan-American conference of 1881, 52
Pan-American Union, 8, 127
Paris, Treaty of (1898), 90
Paris peace conference. See Versailles, Treaty of

INDEX

INDEX

Seward, William H., 7, 14, 31, 81, 109, 178, 179
Sherman, John, 181
Sino-Japanese War, 18, 93–94, 145
Smith, Robert, 180
Somoza, Anastasio, 35
Soulé, Pierre, 142
Southeast Asia Treaty Organization, 113, 226
South Vietnam, 113, 226, 227
Soviet Union. *See* Russia, Soviet
Spain, 6, 10, 11, 13, 15, 30, 32, 51, 57, 79, 88, 90, 91, 100, 108, 117, 123, 142, 166, 169, 175, 201, 202
Spanish-American War, 2, 14–15, 31, 32, 57, 63, 90, 99, 101, 102, 103, 104, 105, 106, 123, 130, 143, 147, 148, 169, 171, 173, 194, 202
Stalin, Joseph, 70, 214, 220, 222, 223
Stassen, Harold, 203
State, Department of, 37, 43, 46, 59, 61, 89, 92, 140, 157, 163, 174, 178, 179, 181–183, 184, 185, 186, 197, 210
State, Secretary of, 157, 178–181, 183, 185, 198–199
Stimson, Henry L., 19
Stimson doctrine, 93
Study of War, A, 119
Sudetenland, 85
Sumner, Charles, 89, 199

Taft, William Howard, 170, 175; administration, 21, 36, 57, 58, 60, 144, 181, 190
Taft-Katsura memorandum (1905), 91
Tariff Commission, 183
Tariff policies, U.S., 24, 52–54, 60–61, 145, 151, 153, 164, 195
Tax policies, U.S., 68
Taylor, Zachary, 101, 123, 142, 170, 173, 175; administration, 80
Teheran conference (1943), 218
Texas, acquisition of, 7, 11, 13, 100, 141, 167, 194, 202, 209
Thailand, 113, 226

Tojo, Hideki, 105, 172
Trinidad, fortification of, 26, 164
Tripolitan War, 50, 167
Trujillo, Rafael Leonidas, 35, 88–89
Truman, Harry S., 96, 97, 106, 163, 168, 173, 185, 204, 219, 220
Turkey, 51, 118, 163, 194, 200, 204, 223, 224, 226
Tyler, John, 175; administration, 141, 167

U-2 incident, 213, 225
United Nations, 40, 173, 205, 211, 215, 216, 231; Assembly, 88, 96, 219; Charter, 106, 113, 127, 182, 195, 203, 220, 223; Security Council, 134, 204; Secretary General, 135

Van Buren, Martin, 170, 175; administration, 141
Vandenberg, Arthur, 200, 203, 204, 206
Vatican, 175
Venezuela, 28; dispute with British Guiana, 7, 9, 109, 126, 143
Vera Cruz, 36
Versailles, Treaty of, 17, 23–24, 85–86, 111, 175, 190–191, 192, 193, 200, 202, 206, 209, 210, 211, 215
Virgin Islands, 31, 34, 43
Vishinsky, Andrei, 223

Walker, William, 142
War of 1812, 4, 62, 99, 101, 102, 103, 105, 107, 117, 122, 130, 131, 140, 142, 147, 148, 171, 201, 206
Washington, Declaration of (1942), 3, 167
Washington, George, 5, 170, 174; administration, 3, 4, 50, 62, 78, 105, 159, 160, 161, 162, 163, 201
Washington conference (1889), 8
Washington conference (1921–1922), 17, 19, 24, 56, 66, 109, 132, 145, 202, 209–210, 211. *See also* Nine-Power Treaty
Webster, Daniel, 14, 80–81, 142, 179

[246]

INDEX

Webster-Ashburton Treaty (1842), 12, 62, 141, 209
Welles, Sumner, 182
Western Europe, 87, 224, 225, 229. *See also* Europe
Whig Party, 62, 128, 142, 201, 206
White, Edward D., 110
Willkie, Wendell, 25, 177, 203
Wilson, Woodrow, 95, 170; and World War I, 17, 21–24, 25, 63, 64–66, 83–86, 93, 124, 171–172; and Mexico, 36, 46, 57, 82, 160; administration, 60, 90, 111, 113, 114–115, 127, 144, 145, 148, 163, 168, 169, 176, 178–179, 181, 191, 200, 206–207, 208, 211
Wood, Gen. Leonard, 33
World Court, 127; protocol, 190, 191, 192
World Decision, The, 110
World War I, 16–17, 21–23, 25, 27, 36, 55, 60, 63–66, 83–86, 92–93, 99, 101, 102, 104, 112, 130, 131, 144, 147, 153, 169, 174, 190, 194, 202, 210, 215; U.S. entry, 105, 106, 109–110, 123–124, 145, 148, 163, 171–172
World War II, 1, 3, 8, 20, 25–26, 27, 40, 55, 95, 99, 101, 102, 103, 114, 115, 130, 131, 132, 133, 146, 147, 153, 163, 194, 196, 203, 210, 217, 218; U.S. entry, 104, 105, 106, 112, 124–125, 148, 171, 202
Wright, Quincy, 119
Wriston, Henry, 163

XYZ affair, 101, 138

Yalta conference, 92, 174, 218, 219, 223, 224
Young Plan (1929), 24, 60
Yucatan, 7, 31
Yugoslavia, 229

Zionism, 215